Essential Series

T0183838

Springer

London
Berlin
Heidelberg
New York
Barcelona
Hong Kong
Milan
Paris
Singapore
Tokyo

Also in this series:

John Cowell
Essential Visual Basic 5.0 *fast*
3-540-76148-9

Duncan Reed and Peter Thomas
Essential HTML *fast*
3-540-76199-3

John Hunt
Essential JavaBeans *fast*
1-85233-032-5

John Vince
Essential Virtual Reality *fast*
1-85233-012-0

John Cowell
Essential Visual J++ 6.0 *fast*
1-85233-013-9

John Cowell
Essential Java 2 *fast*
1-85233-071-6

John Cowell
Essential Visual Basic 6.0 *fast*
1-85233-071-6

Ian Chivers
Essential Visual C++ 6.0 *fast*
1-85233-170-4

John Vince
Essential Computer Animation *fast*
1-85233-141-0

Aladdin Ayesh
Essential Dynamic HTML *fast*
1-85233-626-9

David Thew
Essential Access 2000 *fast*
1-85233-295-6

Ian Palmer
Essential Java 3D *fast*
1-85233-394-4

Matthew Norman
Essential ColdFusion *fast*
1-85233-315-4

Ian Chivers
Essential Linux *fast*
1-85233-408-8

Fiaz Hussain
Essential Flash 5.0 *fast*
1-85233-451-7

John Vince
Essential Mathematics for
Computer Graphics *fast*
1-85233-380-4

Aladdin Ayesh
Essential UML *fast*
1-85233-413-4

John Cowell

Essential VB .NET *fast*

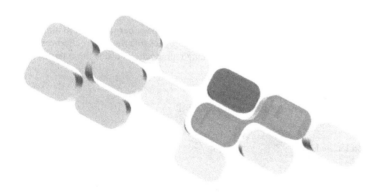

 Springer

Author and Series Editor
John Cowell, BSc (Hons), MPhil, PhD
Department of Computer Science, De Montfort University, The Gateway,
Leicester LE1 9BH

British Library Cataloguing in Publication Data
Cowell, John, 1957-
   Essential VB .NET fast. – (Essential series)
   1. Visual programming languages (Computer science)
   2. Internet programming
   I. Title II. VB .NET fast
   005.1'33
ISBN 1852335912

Library of Congress Cataloging-in-Publication Data
A catalog record for this book is available from the Library of Congress

Apart from any fair dealing for the purposes of research or private study, or criticism or review, as
permitted under the Copyright, Designs and Patents Act 1988, this publication may only be
reproduced, stored or transmitted, in any form or by any means, with the prior permission in writing
of the publishers, or in the case of reprographic reproduction in accordance with the terms of licences
issued by the Copyright Licensing Agency. Enquiries concerning reproduction outside those terms
should be sent to the publishers.

ISBN 1-85233-591-2 Springer-Verlag London Berlin Heidelberg
a member of BertelsmannSpringer Science+Business Media GmbH
http://www.springer.co.uk

© Springer-Verlag London Limited 2002
Printed in Great Britain

The use of registered names, trademarks etc. in this publication does not imply, even in the absence
of a specific statement, that such names are exempt from the relevant laws and regulations and
therefore free for general use.

The publisher makes no representation, express or implied, with regard to the accuracy of the
information contained in this book and cannot accept any legal responsibility or liability for any
errors or omissions that may be made.

Typesetting: Electronic text files prepared by the author
Printed and bound at The Cromwell Press, Trowbridge, Wiltshire
34/3830-543210 Printed on acid-free paper SPIN 10866262

Contents

Contents

Chapter 1

Why Use Visual Basic .NET?

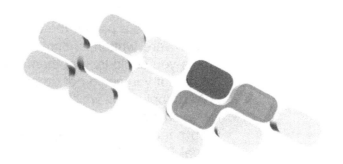

Introduction

Visual Basic .NET is part of the Visual Studio .NET family of products in addition to Visual C++ and the new programming language Visual C#. While the syntax and style of Visual Basic .NET is very similar to earlier versions of Visual Basic this version has many important improvements, which will ensure that Visual Basic remains as Microsoft's most popular Integrated Development Environment (IDE) for application development. Whether you want to develop applications for Windows or for the World Wide Web (WWW) Visual Basic .NET is an excellent tool for producing reliable, professional applications *fast*.

Visual Basic has set the standard as one of the best development environments for Windows applications, but increasingly we want to create applications for the WWW which will run within a browser environment. This version of Visual Basic provides an excellent set of tools for doing this.

The WWW is a part of the Internet and originally Web pages were written in simple HTML and were static, that is you could look at them and follow links to other pages but you could not do anything else. To develop a Web application which can respond to user requests, for example, reading a database, and updating the Web page, other tools apart from HTML are needed. Visual Basic .NET uses an extended version of ASP called ASP.NET for doing this.

There are over three million users of Visual Basic in the world, and with the improvements in this new version Microsoft are sure to increase this number.

What do I need?

Visual Basic .NET needs either the Windows NT 4.0 or later, Windows 2000 or Windows XP operating systems. It demands a fairly recent PC, at least a Pentium II 450MHz and ideally at least a Pentium III 600MHz. It will run with 64Mb for Windows 4.0, 96Mb for Windows 2000, 192Mb for Windows 2000 server and 160 for Windows XP. It will take up at least 500MB of disk space.

If you want to develop Web applications you will need access to a server which has the .NET extensions installed.

The testing of all the examples in this book was carried out on a Pentium 1.5GHz with 256 MB of memory and the Windows XP Professional operating system. The server has 512Mb of memory and uses the Windows 2000 Server operating system.

Why upgrade?

If you are already using an earlier version of Visual Basic and are familiar with it, it can be a difficult decision to decide to go through the upheaval of learning a new version. There are so many extensive changes to Visual Basic .NET that the extra work is definitely worthwhile. The major changes include:

- Support for Microsoft's new .NET framework.
- Tools for creating interactive Web pages using an updated version of Active Server pages (ASP)
- Significant additions to the Visual Basic programming language including object oriented extensions such as classes, inheritance and polymorphism.

- The available data types have changed, for example the **Currency** data type is no longer supported.
- The development of Windows applications has significant changes, including the way control arrays are used and how controls are navigated.
- Some additional controls are available.
- The properties of many standard controls have changed, for example, the **Text** property of a **Label** control replaces the **Caption** property.
- Some new deployment features have been added to assist you in distributing your applications.
- The tools for developing applications which reference a relational database have been improved.

In addition to these major changes there are many minor improvements over previous versions. Microsoft have paid a lot of attention to what software developers want from an Integrated Development Environment (IDE) and have made real improvements on earlier versions.

If you are currently using an earlier version of Visual Basic, you may be concerned about these changes particularly if you have written some large applications in one of these versions. There is an update wizard which will convert projects to the new version, this can be slow for large applications and it often seems to run into problems, which it reports, for you to solve yourself. Opening a project created in an earlier version automatically invokes this wizard.

Is this book for you?

If you are not a current user of Visual Basic you will find that it is a great way of developing robust applications for Windows and the Web. If you are considering upgrading from an earlier version of Visual

Basic, there are many new features in addition to the ability to develop Web applications which make it worthwhile.

This books assumes that you are familiar with using Windows applications, such as spreadsheets and databases, but does not assume that you have any prior knowledge of using Visual Basic or a similar IDE: it is therefore suitable for the beginner. If you have some experience of programming, particularly using an IDE, you will find that this book allows you to speed through the introductory material in the early chapters to the more complex aspects in the later chapters. If you want to learn how to develop applications in Visual Basic, but do not have time to read a 1000 page book, you will find that *Essential VB .NET fast* is an excellent introduction to developing applications for Windows and the Web.

This book does provide an introduction to developing Web based applications, but does not cover this large area in depth.

Visual Basic has an excellent Help system which is useful if you want to know a specific piece of information, but it is not very helpful if you need a structured guide to the IDE and language. Although this book is not huge, it covers everything you need to develop serious applications for Windows and the Web.

How to use this book

This book contains many examples to illustrate the ideas it covers; you can read through from the beginning to the end, but where possible each chapter has been written to be self contained, so that if, for example, you want to find out how to use the object oriented aspects of Visual Basic you can just read that chapter without the need to read the preceding chapters.

If you are unfamiliar with Visual Basic you should start at the beginning and work through the first seven chapters which deal with the basics of the Visual Basic IDE and language, including developing Windows applications.

Chapter 8 covers the object oriented aspects of Visual Basic .NET including how to create and use classes and objects.

Chapter 9 looks at some more controls for Windows applications, which make it easier to write powerful applications.

Chapters 10 and 11 look at how to develop Web applications and some of the most important Web controls.

Chapters 12 to 14 look at using forms and dialogs and how to handle mouse and keyboard events.

Chapters 15 to 17 look at database applications development for Windows applications, in particular: an introduction to SQL; using the Data Form Wizard; and using the DataReader and DataSet classes to browse databases.

This book does not cover every aspect of Visual Basic: if it did it would be ten times its size and take much longer to read. What this book does is focus on the most widely used features of Visual Basic that you need to start to develop Visual Basic applications *fast*.

Don't type!

All of the program examples in this book are available from the Essential Series Web site www.Essential-Series.com – so you don't have to type any program examples. While you are at the site take a look at the other books which are available in the series.

Chapter 2

The Visual Basic .NET IDE

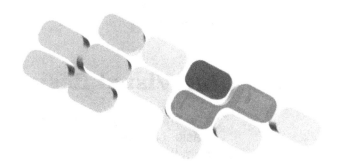

Introduction

The Visual Basic .NET IDE is very powerful, allowing you to create a wide variety of applications, both for Windows and the Web. The problem with this flexibility is that the IDE can initially seem very confusing and the range of options it offers bewildering, but it is very logically organized and in this chapter we are going to look at how the key features of the IDE are organized.

In this chapter we are going to look at:

- The types of applications you can develop.
- The Solution Explorer.
- The design form.
- The Help system.
- The Project Explorer.
- The Toolbox.
- The Properties window.

In the next chapter we will see how to use these features to create user interfaces for Windows applications.

Running Visual Basic

The first thing you need to decide when you run Visual Basic .NET is what sort of project you want to create, from the choices available.

Click on the **Open Project** button or select the **File | New | Project** menu option. The dialog shown in Figure 2.1 is displayed.

The different project types creates a set of template files appropriate to the type of application you want to create.

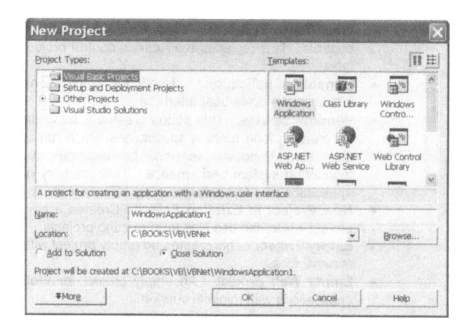

Figure 2.1 *Starting a new project.*

Project types

The main project template types which are available are:

- **Windows Application**. This is used for stand-alone Windows applications. This replaces the Standard EXE project type in earlier versions of Visual Basic.

- **Class Library**. Creates a re-usable class or non-visual control.

- **Windows Control Library**. Used for creating custom controls. This replaces the User Control project type.

- **ASP.NET Web Application**. Used for creating interactive ASP applications.

- **ASP.NET Web Service**. Used to create XML Web services.

- **Web Control Library**. Used for creating custom controls. This replaces the ActiveX control project type.
- **Console Application**. Used for applications without a Windows user interface.
- **Window Service**. This option creates a template for creating long running applications which run in their own Windows session, for example, for monitoring system performance. This category of application was formerly known as NT services.
- **New Project in Existing Folder**. Creates a new project which can use files from existing projects.
- **Empty Project**. This creates an empty project with minimal files.
- **Empty Web project**. An empty project for Web applications with minimal support.

The most commonly used template type are for **Windows Application** and **ASP.NET Web Application** development.

It is unlikely that the last two **Empty Project** options will be often used, since the other templates provide an essential framework for applications development.

If you choose to open an existing project, all of the files in that project are available for you to view or change within the IDE.

All of the files in a Visual Basic application are contained within a project. When you start to create an application you need to create a new project. To continue work on an existing application you must open its project file.

The Visual Basic .NET IDE

The appearance of the IDE varies depending on the project type which you select, you can also customize how it appears. We are going to look at the IDE when the Windows Application type is selected. Most of the components are also found in the other project types. The components which we are going to look at are:

- The Solution Explorer and Class View.
- The Help system.
- The Windows Form Designer.
- The Toolbox.
- The Properties window.

Toolbox   Windows Form Designer   Solution Explorer   Properties Window

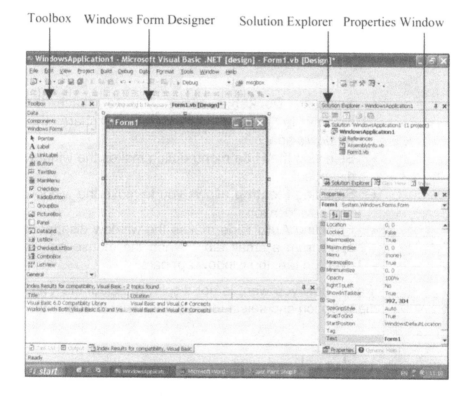

Figure 2.2 *The Visual Basic IDE.*

Note that the appearance of your system may appear to be different from the one shown in Figure 2.2. Most windows, such as the Properties window can appear as stand-alone windows or can be docked to share space with other windows – so that they can be selected by using tags at the bottom of the window. In

Figure 2.2, the Properties window shares space with the Dynamic Help window, and the Solution Explorer shares space with the Class View and Index windows. If you wish to change how a window is displayed right click on the title bar of the window to display the speed menu shown in Figure 2.3.

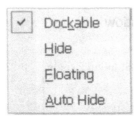

Figure 2.3 *The speed menu.*

- Selecting **Dockable** allows you to attach the window to another window, or to share that window's space.
- Selecting the **Hide** menu option makes the window disappear.
- Selecting **Floating** allows you to move the window to a new location.
- Selecting **Auto Hide** makes the window disappear apart from a small tab. When the mouse moves over the tab, the window appears.

If a window you want is not displayed select the **View** menu option and select the item you want to see.

The Solution Explorer

One of the problems with writing a large application which has a lot of files, is finding the file you want. There are two ways of moving easily around an application. The Solution Explorer displays a list of all the files in your application and the Class View displays a list of all the symbols in your application, such as classes, methods, functions and modules. They are shown in Figure 2.4.

View code   View designer   Class view: sort by type

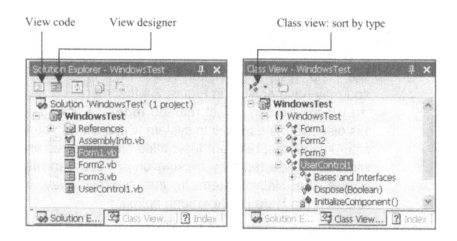

Figure 2.4 *The Solution Explorer and the Class View.*

These two windows may be displayed as separate windows or they may be superimposed on each other as shown in Figure 2.4. You can switch between them by clicking on the tag at the bottom of the window. To move to a form or any other item double click on its name.

All forms have a visual aspect as well as some background Visual Basic code which is used for handling events which occur on that form. Using the two icons shown at the top of the Solutions Explorer on the left of Figure 2.4 you can switch between these two views.

The button at the top of the Class View window shown on the right of Figure 2.4 allows you to choose the order in which the items are listed, you can choose either : **Sort Alphabetically**; **Sort by Type**; **Sort by Access**; **Group by Type**.

The Help system

The Help system in Visual Basic .NET is excellent. You may have noticed in Figure 2.4 that there is a third tag which you can select marked **Index**. Clicking on this displays the usual Help system which allows you to enter key words: relevant topic titles are displayed and you can view a topic by clicking on it. You can also access the Help system in the standard way by selecting the **Help | Index** menu option.

A very useful feature of the Visual Basic .NET Help system is the Dynamic Help facility, shown in Figure 2.5.

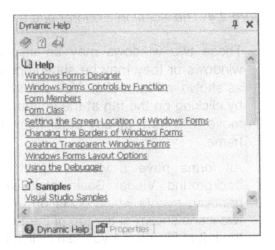

Figure 2.5 Dynamic Help.

This provides context-sensitive help relevant to what you are doing at any time, if for example you click on a button on a form the dynamic help automatically changes to topics relevant to buttons.

The Windows Form Designer

Most applications in Visual Basic have at least one window or form which may display information or accept input. When you start most types of projects you have a design form to work in.

You can change the size of a form by dragging one of the black squares at the edge of the form as shown in Figure 2.6. The size of the form at design–time is the same as its size when the application runs, although you can resize a form at run–time by writing some Visual Basic instructions or by dragging one of the edges of the form in the usual way.

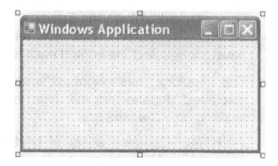

Figure 2.6 The Windows Form Designer.

By default there is a grid of dots over the form; when you add controls such as buttons and labels to the form they automatically snap to the nearest grid dot and adjust their size so that their width and height correspond to an integer number of grid dots. This is a useful feature since it helps you to line up your controls and gives a professional look to your applications. You can turn this feature off for a particular form by selecting that form and changing the **SnapToGrid** property in the Properties Window to **False**. If you want to change this property for all forms in the application or change the spacing between the grid squares select the **Tool | Options** menu option and select the **Windows Form Designer**.

The Toolbox

If you want to add a control to a form you must first select that control from the Toolbox. Then move to the design form and drag the mouse. The position where you first press the left mouse button when you start dragging is anchored and becomes one of the corners of the control. If you want to add another control you must select it from the Toolbox and repeat the process. If you want to add more than one control of the same type press the Ctrl button while selecting the control you wish to add from the Toolbox. You can now add as many controls of that type as you wish without having to reselect the control each time.

The Toolbox has eight different tabs, the tabs displayed depend on the type of project you are working on. The tabs are:

- **HTML**: Contains a set of controls which can be used on Web pages, such as **Label** and **Button** controls.
- **Data**: Contains a variety of data objects for database applications, for example for providing a connection to a data source.
- **Components**: A set of controls for systems functions such as monitoring access to a file or logging performance. You can add your own user-defined controls to this tab.
- **XML Schema**: XML Schema documents define and validate XML data. This tab displays elements you can add to XML schemas.
- **Clipboard Ring**: Displays the last twelve items added to the system using the cut and paste commands.

- **Web Forms**: Controls used for creating Web pages.
- **Windows Forms**: A set of controls used for creating Windows applications.
- **General**: Initially this tab contains only the pointer tool, but it is intended to store custom tools.

Figure 2.7 shows the **HTML**, **Web Forms** and **Windows Forms** tabs which are the most commonly used.

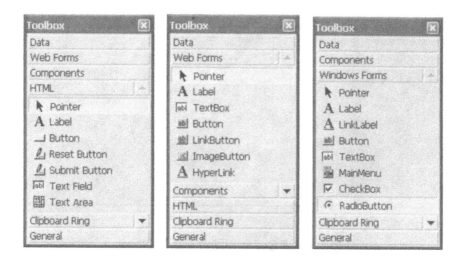

Figure 2.7 The Toolbox.

We will look in detail at many of the controls from the Toolbox.

Adding custom controls

In addition to the controls available on the Toolbox many others are supplied by Microsoft with Visual Basic .NET which you can install. There are also many custom controls available at low cost. If you are starting work on a major application it is worthwhile checking third party suppliers on the Web to see if useful controls are available.

To install new controls select the **Tools | Customize Toolbox** menu option as shown in Figure 2.8.

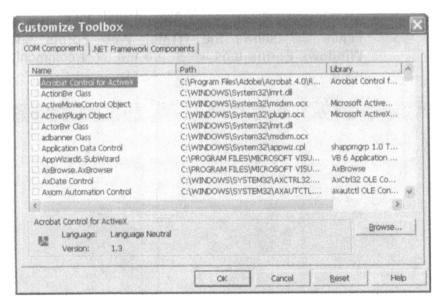

Figure 2.8 *Customizing the Toolbox.*

There are two tags for adding both COM and .NET controls. COM controls may be used in Windows applications while .NET controls are used for Web based applications. When you check an item and click the **OK** button an icon representing it appears on the appropriate Toolbox tag.

You can customize the grouping of controls on the Toolbox or even create a new tag. Right clicking on the Toolbox gives a range of options which cover every possibility.

The Properties window

Every control in your application has a set of properties which control the position of the control, its size, the font it uses to display text and so on. If you select a control, its properties are displayed in the Properties window.

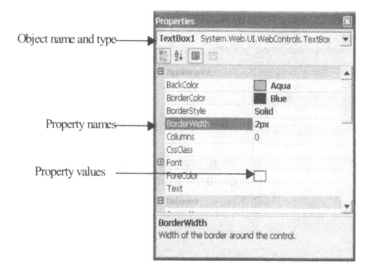

Figure 2.9 *The Properties window.*

Figure 2.9 shows the Properties window for a **TextBox** control from the **Web Forms** tab. The buttons at the top of the window vary depending on what type of application is being produced and what control has been selected.

The most often used ones are shown in Table 2.1.

Table 2.1 Buttons in the Properties window.

Button	Description
	Groups the properties into categories, for example, all of the properties related to appearance.
	List the properties alphabetically.
	Right click and select **Description** to display a brief description of the selected property underneath the list of properties.
	Displays the Property Page dialog which gives details of a selected Project or Solution, such as the name of the startup object. This button is disabled if a Project or Solution is not selected in the Solution Explorer.

In the next chapter we are going to take a closer look at the controls found on the Windows Forms tab of the Toolbox.

Chapter 3

Windows Controls

Introduction

There are two main categories of applications which can be developed in Visual Basic .NET, those which run in a Windows environment and those which run in a Web environment. The controls which each of these applications use are similar, but there are some important differences, even for controls as simple as buttons.

In this chapter we are going to look at:

- How to add Windows controls to a form.
- Selecting, moving and resizing controls.
- Changing properties.
- Some common Windows controls.
- Principles of user interface design.

Adding controls to a window

If you want to experiment with the controls described in this chapter select the **File | New Project** menu option and select the **Windows Application** option from the **New Project** dialog.

This application will automatically have one window, which will be displayed when you run the application.

You can run your application immediately after creating it – select the **Debug | Start** menu option or click the **Start** icon shown in Figure 3.1.

      Figure 3.1 The Start icon.

To add a control to a window, select the control in the Toolbox and then move to the window where you want to add the control. Drag the mouse to draw the control: the position where you start to drag will become one corner of the control. Do not worry if the control is not in the correct position or is the wrong size, it is easy to change these things at any time. By default the control will be aligned to the grid dots which are shown on the window.

Selecting controls

In the Toolbox all of the icons except for one represent different controls: the Selection tool which is used to select one or more controls you have placed on a window.

When you have added a control to a form, the Selection tool is automatically re-selected in the Toolbox.

If you want to add more than one control of the same type you must select that control again in the Toolbox and repeat the process. If you wish to add several controls of the same type you can press the Ctrl button as you select the control you want to add from the Toolbox. The type of control you choose in the Toolbox remains selected until you explicitly select another control type.

There are two ways of selecting a control which you have placed on a form:

- Click on that control. When you click on another control the first is de-selected. To select more than one control keep the Ctrl button pressed when you click on the controls.
- Press the left mouse button and drag, a dotted box appears, when you release the mouse button all controls wholly or partially within the dotted box are selected.

Moving and resizing controls

To select a control you have placed on a form, click on it. If you want to change the size of the control, select it by clicking on it and then dragging one of the handles as shown in Figure 3.2.

Figure 3.2 *Selecting, resizing and moving controls.*

You can move a control by selecting it, pressing the mouse on it and dragging.

Changing properties

Every control has a set of properties. The value of these properties determines every aspect of the control's behaviour. Some properties can only be changed at run–time, that is when the application is executing, but the majority can be changed at both run–time and design–time. To change the properties of a control, select it. Its properties are displayed in the Properties window. If you cannot see the Properties window select the **View | Properties Window** menu option or press **F4**.

The type of the control and its name are displayed in a TextBox at the top of the Properties window.

To change a property of a control, select the control and click on that property in the Properties window. There are three different ways of changing property values:

- Typing the value of the new property. The **Text** property, for example, contains the text which is displayed in a **Label** control. Whatever text you type is automatically shown in that control.

Click here to
display the
Font dialog

 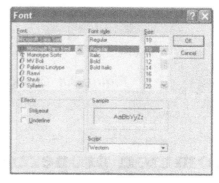

Figure 3.3 Changing the **Font** property.

- Some properties have a button with three dots adjacent to the property value; clicking on this button displays a dialog. The **Font** property is an example of this type. Clicking on this button displays the Font dialog as shown in Figure 3.3.

Select the property values you want from the dialog and press the **OK** button.

- Some properties have a few options which are displayed in a list so that you can select the value you want. The **BackColor** property is an example of this type of property as shown in Figure 3.4. Clicking on the down arrow displays the menu (which may be a selection of colour or text) and you can choose the value that you want for this property.

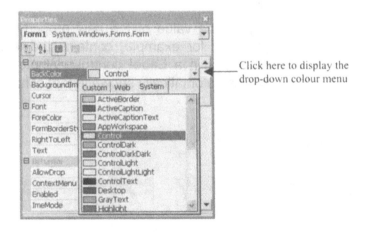

Figure 3.4 *Changing the* **BackColor** *property.*

Common properties

One of the major concerns for programmers who are unused to using a Windows IDE is that there are so many properties for the controls. Fortunately many of the properties are common to many controls and are used in the same way. Most applications require a small set of the available properties which you will quickly learn.

The following properties are common to most of the controls which are visible at run–time.

- The **Name** property is used by Visual Basic to uniquely identify each control. If you want you can rely on the default names created by Visual Basic, for example *Label1*, *Label2* and so on, but for serious applications it is usually best to give controls your own meaningful names.
- If the **Enabled** property is **True** the control is available for use at run–time. If it is **False** it is disabled and appears "greyed out".
- The **Visible** property is **True** if the control can be seen. An invisible control is also disabled.
- The **Font** property determines the type and size of the font used to display text.
- The **BackColor** property gives the colour of the background of the control.

There are some common properties which are handled differently at design and run-time:

- At design time, the **Size.Height** and **Size.Width** properties determine the size of the control. At run-time these properties may be used to read the values but not set them. The **Height** and **Width** properties however, may be used both to read and set them. For example, at run time the height of a control called *OKButton* is given by both *OKButton*.**Size**.**Height** and *OKButton*.**Height**, but the first cannot be assigned a value, so if you wish to change the height at run-time the **Height** property must be used not the **Size.Height** property. Similarly the **Size.Width** property can be read but not assigned, while the **Size** property can be both read and assigned.
- In a similar way at design time the position of the top left corner of the control is determined by the **Location.X** and **Location.Y** properties. At run-time these properties may be used to read the

values but to change them the **Top** and **Left** properties must be used.

Some controls such as the **Timer** control, which informs your application when a specified amount of time has elapsed, are not visible at run–time and consequently have a very restricted (but adequate) set of properties.

The Label control

The simplest of the controls in the Windows Forms tab of the Toolbox is the **Label** control.

This control is usually used to display text or images which do not change while the application is running, although if you wish you can use a **Label** control to display a status message indicating the progress of a lengthy activity.

Properties of the Label control

To change the text displayed change the **Text** property.

If the **AutoSize** property is **True**, the control will expand horizontally to fit the text to be displayed. Note that you will not be able to manually resize the control by dragging if this property is **True**. If the **AutoSize** property is **False**, the control remains the same size and automatically wraps on to the next line when a line is full, however some of the text may not be visible.

The position of the text within **Label** is determined by the **TextAlign** property which offers one of nine possible positions as shown in Figure 3.5.

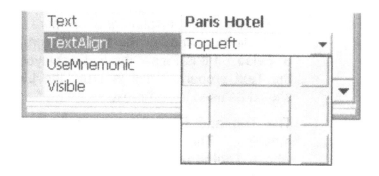

Figure 3.5 *Changing the **TextAlign** property.*

To display an image use the **Image** property. You can use the **ImageList** and **ImageIndex** properties to attach a list of images to the control. The **Image** property cannot be used at the same time as the **ImageList** and **ImageIndex** properties. For example, the code shown below creates an **ImageList**, changes its default size from 16×16, to 30×30 and adds two images to it. The **ImageList** property of a **Label** called *lblLabel* is assigned this new **ImageList**. The **ImageIndex** property is set to zero, so that the first of the two images in the **ImageList** object is displayed. Setting it to one displays the second image in the list.

```
Dim imageList1 As New ImageList( )
    imageList1.ImageSize = New Size(30, 30)
    imageList1.Images.Add(Image.FromFile("c:\Holiday\Paris\Arc.bmp"))
    imageList1.Images.Add(Image.FromFile("c:\ Holiday\Paris\Tower.bmp"))
    lblLabel.ImageList = imageList1
    lblLabel.ImageIndex = 0
```

The TextBox control

The **TextBox** control can be used to display text in a manner similar to the **Label** control. The key difference is that text can be typed into a **TextBox** and edited at run–time.

A **TextBox** can display one or more lines of text depending on whether the **MultiLine** property is **True** or **False**. If it is **False,** the text displayed is set using the **Text** property. If it is **True,** the **Lines** property should be used to enter text.

The Tab and Return keys usually have a special meaning. The Tab key moves to another control whose **TabIndex** value is the next in the sequence. The Return key carries out the action of clicking on a default button which is specified in the **AcceptButton** property of the Form. If you want to input text into a **TextBox** it is often useful to override this and allow the Return and Tab keys to be typed into the TextBox. To do this, set the **AcceptsTab** and **AcceptsReturn** properties to **True**. If **AcceptsTab** is **True** to move the focus to the next control you must press Ctrl+Tab. If **AcceptsReturn** is **False** you must type Ctrl+Return to go to a new line. However, if the **AcceptsReturn** property of the Form is not assigned to a button, the Return key moves to the next line in the **TextBox** irrespective of the state of the **AcceptsReturn** property.

Another useful property of the **TextBox** which determines its behaviour is the **WordWrap** property. If set to **True** the text is moved to the next line when the current line is the width of the **TextBox**.

An application with two textboxes is shown in Figure 3.6.

There are some unexpected interactions with the properties of **TextBox** controls which you need to watch, for example, if the **WordWrap** property is **True** a horizontal scroll bar will not be displayed even if you request it using the **ScrollBars** property.

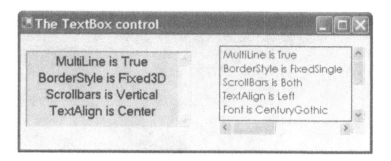

*Figure 3.6 The **TextBox** control.*

The **MaxLength** property of this control can be rather confusing. It is the maximum number of characters you can type at run-time – you can enter more than this at design time. It is useful if you wish to limit the number of characters input, for example a password. This can be used in conjunction with the **PasswordChar** property. If this is set to any character, apart from a null, whatever you type that character will appear, although the actual text typed will be available to your application. The usual character used is *. Another curious interaction between properties is that if the **MultiLine** property is set to true the **PasswordChar** property is ignored.

The PictureBox control

The **PictureBox** control is used to display pictures. The **Image** property is used to specify the image. Most common graphics formats are supported including bitmap, icon, enhanced metafile, JPEG and GIF.

Figure 3.7 shows this control. The three images are all the same size, resolution and format, but they are displayed differently because of the **SizeMode** and **BorderStyle** properties.

Figure 3.7 *The **PictureBox** control.*

The **SizeMode** property has one of four values:

- **AutoSize**: The **PictureBox** is resized to fit the picture.
- **CenterImage**: If the **PictureBox** is larger than the picture, the whole image is displayed centrally positioned. If the image is larger then only the central portion is displayed.
- **Normal**: The top left of the picture is positioned at the top left corner of the control.
- **StretchImage**: The picture is resized so that it fits exactly within the control.

The **BorderStyle** property can be either **None**, **FixedSingle** or **Fixed3D**.

The CheckBox, RadioButton and GroupBox controls

We are going to look at these three controls together, since they are often used with each other.

The difference between the **RadioButton** and **CheckBox** controls is that the **RadioButtons** behave as a group in which only one can be checked, whenever a **RadioButton** is checked all the others in the group are unchecked. To group **RadioButtons** they must be placed within a container such as a **Panel**, **GroupBox** or **Form**. The **GroupBox** control consists of a box with an optional title.

In Figure 3.8, four **RadioButton** controls have been placed within a **GroupBox**. The **Text** property of the **GroupBox** provides the caption. The **Text** property of the **RadioButton** and **CheckBox** controls provides the text adjacent to those controls. The **GroupBox** and the controls within it behave as a single unit and when you select and move the **GroupBox** all of the controls it contains are also moved.

All three of these controls in common with forms have the **BackgroundImage** property which can be used to display an interesting picture. In Figure 3.8, this property has been used for the form. In addition, the **RadioButton** and **CheckBox** controls have an **Image** property which allows a further image to be displayed.

You can only select one of the **RadioButtons**, but you can select any number of the **CheckBox** controls.

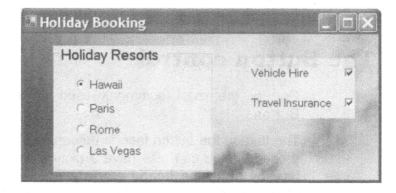

Figure 3.8 *The **RadioButton**, **GroupBox** and* *CheckBox controls.*

The position of the text relative to the button is determined by the **CheckAlign** property. This has nine possible values. The default value used for the **RadioButtons** is **middle left**. For the **CheckBox** controls in Figure 3.8 this has been changed to **middle right**.

There are three properties which affect the state of a **CheckBox**:

- The **ThreeState** property. This is either **True** or **False**. If **True,** the checked state can be one of three values. If **False,** (the default) the checked state can only be one of two possible values.
- The **CheckedState** property. Can be either **True** or **False**. If the **ThreeState** property is **True** it may also be **Indeterminate** and appears to be greyed out.
- The **Checked** property can be either **True** or **False**. If the **CheckedState** property is **True** or **Indeterminate** it is **True**. If **CheckedState** is **False** it is **False**.

If the **ThreeState** property is **True** successive clicks on the button move between the three possible states.

The **RadioButton** control only has the **Checked** property.

The Button control

One of the most commonly–used controls is the **Button**.

The text on the button face is determined by the **Text** property. You can also have a picture on the button face by using the **Image** property. In common with other controls you can display a variety of images using the **ImageIndex** and **ImageList** properties, but this requires some Visual Basic code to be written.

The position of the displayed image is determined by
the **ImageAlign** property which behaves in a similar
way to the **TextAlign** property.

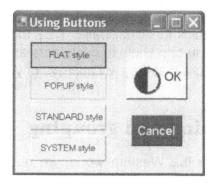

Figure 3.9 The *Button* control.

Figure 3.9 shows a variety of **Button** controls, the
FlatStyle property has four possible values: **Flat**,
Popup, **Standard** and **System** which alters the
appearance but leaves the behaviour of the control the
same. You can also change both the **ForeColor** (the
text) and the **BackColor** (the background) properties.
An unusual interaction between the properties is that
the **ForeColor** and **BackColor** properties are ignored
if the **FlatStyle** property is set to **System**.

Creating a good user interface

The most successful applications which are a pleasure
to use have good user interfaces, that is they are
visually attractive, the text and menus have meaningful
names and the application is logically organized.
Visual Basic .NET has the ability to produce any
Windows user interface that you want.

To create a great user interface takes a lot of practice,
but you can get very good results by following a few
simple guidelines for the positioning of controls and

consistency by using the same colour scheme and font throughout the interface.

It is important to consider your target audience when designing your user interface. It is straightforward and quick in Visual Basic .NET to create prototypes which you can show to customers and get feedback to make sure that they will approve of your final design.

Positioning and grouping

In the Western world, we read from left to right and from top to bottom, so it is good practice to follow this ordering when designing forms, for example the first pieces of information which have to be supplied in many applications are the name and address, therefore these should be placed in the top left. The implied sequence in which they are filled in should reflect a logical grouping.

Controls which are to be used last should be in the bottom right of the form. This includes buttons such as *OK* or *Cancel*, which are used to proceed to the next stage of the application when the current form has been fully completed.

If a number of controls have a related function it is good to group them together to emphasize this. The grouping can be achieved by placing a box around them or leaving a small amount of white space between them compared to the space between them and other controls.

Consistency

It is visually pleasing if an application is consistent. Individual forms should use controls in the same style, for example, buttons should be the same size. The same font size should be used throughout apart from special cases where you want to emphasize the text. If you have more than one form in your application make sure that the same styles are applied to all of the forms.

It is often possible to use more than one control to fulfil a particular function, for example a **ComboBox** and a **ListBox** control can often be used interchangeably, however to achieve an attractive user interface try to stick with one type throughout the application.

Colours and font size

The choice of colours and fonts has a major impact on the appearance of an application. If you use too many colours, forms can appear chaotic, but this is one situation where you have to consider the target audience carefully. An application for the MTV Web site will have a very different target audience to an application for a company of accountants and consequently different colours and fonts will be appropriate. These aspects of an application are critical to its success, but they are also quick to change, so it is important to create a prototype and show it to the client. Even the most non-technical person knows whether he likes an interface and you are sure to get some positive or negative comments which will allow you to make improvements.

When choosing colours and fonts, the overriding consideration is clarity. Many users may not have an advanced graphics card in their computer and therefore will not be able to view the subtle differences between similar colours, so try to use colours which will be easily distinguished even with a cheap graphics card and monitor.

Not all users will have perfect vision and many will be colour-blind, so choose colours which can be identified by the large majority of people.

A sans-serif font is usually used for headers and a serif font for the rest of the text. Unfortunately, many computers only have a limited range of fonts, so it is best to stick to the most common ones if you are not sure of the capabilities of the computer which will run your application. The most common fonts are Arial which is a sans-serif font and Times Roman which is a serif font. If a computer does not have the font which your application requests the computer will choose something similar, and the results may not be exactly what you had expected. When choosing the font size make sure that it is sufficiently large to be read easily by users. Applications which cause eye strain are very unpopular.

Images

Images can be an effective way of conveying information, but they can take up a lot of disk space and can be slow to load. When you are considering whether to use an image or not you must decide what information the image is conveying and if it could be conveyed more succinctly using a few words of text. Icons are 16×16 pixels and it is difficult to create icons which are meaningful to users, fortunately icons can be bought very cheaply to cover any requirement.

Making choices

When an application runs, the user can enter information into **TextBox** control, select information from lists and **click** on Button controls, but in addition to this there may be many other options available, for example closing the application, using a Help system, or other features. These are usually accessed by a menu system which is covered in Chapter 12.

Chapter 4

Windows Applications

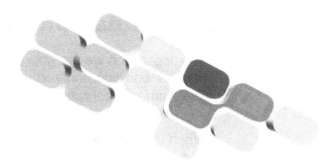

Introduction

Using the controls we have looked at you can create Windows applications with a professional appearance, but, so far, these impressive looking forms do not do anything. All of the controls which we have used have a set of properties associated with them. We have seen how these can be changed at design-time using the Properties window. In addition, these can be changed at run-time. Controls also have a set of events which occur when something happens to the control, such as clicking on a button or selecting an item from a list. To respond to these events you need to write some Visual Basic code. Fortunately the Visual Basic IDE provides an excellent framework for this. In this chapter we are going to develop a working application which changes some changes to control properties at run-time and handles some events.

Showing holiday pictures

The application we are going to develop shows holiday pictures and you can zoom in and out of the picture. The running application is shown in Figure 4.1. Can you guess where this photograph was taken?

When the application is first run, no image is displayed and only the button with the caption *Choose Image* is enabled, that is the other two buttons are not working and their text will appear in a faint grey.

Click on this button and select a file from the dialog. The chosen file is displayed in the **PictureBox** control.

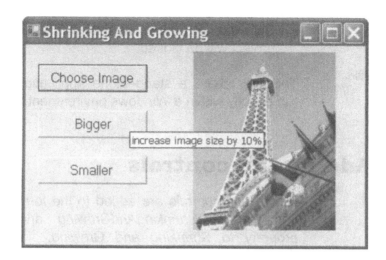

Figure 4.1 *The running application.*

The remaining two buttons are now enabled and the image can be made 10% bigger or smaller by clicking on these two buttons. When the mouse is moved over any of the buttons a helpful message is displayed.

We are going to look at every stage required to develop this application.

By the way if you thought that the question about where the photograph was taken was too easy, it is not the Eiffel Tower in Paris, but its cousin in Las Vegas.

Creating a new project

The first stage is to create a new project for this application:

- Select the **File | New | Project** menu entry.
- Choose **Windows Application** from the New Project dialog displayed.
- Type where you want your project to be stored in the **Name** and **Location** fields.

- Click the **OK** button. By default, the currently open project will be closed.

This will create a stand–alone application which will run directly within a Windows environment.

Adding the controls

Before any controls are added to the form change its name to *frmShrinkingAndGrowing* and its **Text** property to *Shrinking and Growing*. This text is displayed on the title bar.

If you cannot find any elements of the environment, such as the Toolbox, use the **View** menu to specify the item you want to display, or the icons on the standard tool bar. To add the controls:

- Click on the **Button** icon and place the three **Button** controls in turn onto the form. You can either click on the icon and place the first button on the form and repeat this process for the other buttons or you can use a shortcut. If you press the Ctrl button at the same time as you click on the icon you can add as many **Button** controls as you wish without having to select the icon every time.
- Add a **PictureBox** control to the form.
- Next we need to add a control which we have not met yet called the **OpenFileDialog** control. It does not matter where you put it, since it is always placed in the tray at the bottom of the Windows Form Designer and is invisible at run–time. Even though it cannot be seen, it has a set of properties and methods which can be used.
- Finally we add a **ToolTip** control which allows us to display helpful text when the mouse rests on a control. The **ToolTip** control like the **OpenFileDialog** is invisible at run-time and is

placed in the tray beneath the Windows Form Designer.

Completing the user-interface

All of the required controls have been added to the form. Before writing any Visual Basic code we need to rename the controls we have added:

- Change the **Name** property of the top button to *btnOpenFile* and its **Text** property to *Choose Image*.
- Change the **Name** property of the middle button to *btnBigger* and its **Text** property to *Bigger*.
- Change the **Name** property of the final button to *btnSmaller* and its **Text** property to *Smaller.*
- Change the **Name** property of the **PictureBox** control to *picHoliday.*
- Change the name of the *ToolTip1* to *ttTip1.*
- Change the **Name** of the **OpenFileDialog** control to *OpnImageFile.*
- Change the **ToolTip on ttTip1** property of the three buttons to *select an image from the dialog* for the top button, *increase image size by 10%* and *decrease image size by 10%* for the other two buttons. This text will be automatically displayed when the mouse rests on one of these controls.

To improve the appearance of the application, the fonts used have been changed:

- Press the Ctrl button and select all of the buttons.
- Click on the **Font** property in the Properties window and change the font to **MS Sans Serif**; change the size to 12 point in the Font dialog.

This is the point at which it is best to resize and move the controls to their correct positions. Your complete form should look like the one shown in Figure 4.2.

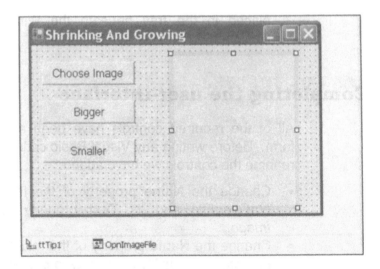

Figure 4.2 *The completed form at design–time.*

The names chosen for the controls may seem rather long, however the reason for the prefixes is that they enable us to identify immediately what type a control is. It is straightforward to do this in an application with one form and a few controls, but in a large application with many forms and hundreds of controls it can be a serious problem. There is a naming convention for controls which should be applied to all controls and variables which we look at in detail in the next chapter.

Handling events

If you run the application, the form appears but the buttons do not do anything. To make them functional we need to write some Visual Basic instructions. In a Windows environment, whenever you take some action such as clicking on a **Button** control, an event occurs. The Visual Basic application detects that event and executes an event handler, which is a collection of Visual Basic instructions. You can add your own Visual Basic code to the event procedure to take some action. For example, when the *Choose Image* **Button** control is clicked an open file dialog is displayed.

The Form Load event handler

The first event we are going to look at is the **Click** event for the top **Button** control. Whenever it is clicked, this event handler is executed.

At this stage in the application the Solution Explorer should be similar to Figure 4.3.

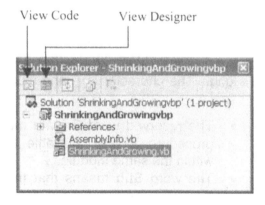

Figure 4.3 *The Solution Explorer.*

For every form there is a corresponding set of event procedures, which are contained in a single module. Every form has its own module which contains its own event procedures. To write the event procedure click on *ShrinkingAndGrowing.vb* and click on the **View Code** icon on the Solution Explorer. You can return to the design form by clicking on the **View Designer** icon which is adjacent to it. The focus of the application is now on the code window.

There are two drop down lists at the top of the code window:

- The left list gives all of the controls available on this form. Select the **Button** control called *btnBigger*.
- The right list gives all the events which the selected control can produce. In this case we want to work with the **Click** event.

Visual Basic now creates the outline event procedure for this event handler:

```
Private Sub btnBigger_Click(ByVal eventSender As System.Object, _
    ByVal eventArgs As System.EventArgs) Handles btnBigger.Click
        ...
    statements
        ...
End Sub
```

Note the use of the continuation character at the end of the first line. You can use this wherever a line is very long. The character is _ and must be preceded by a space.

- The reserved word **Private** means that this event procedure is only available to other procedures within the same module.
- The word **Sub** means that this is the start of an event handler or procedure (this is an historical hangover and stands for subroutine). An event handler or procedure is a collection of statements which has a name and can be treated as a block of code.
- The name of the event handler comes next. This is always made up of the name of the control, an underscore and the name of the event. The open and close brackets are mandatory. In some procedures, information can be passed to the procedure within the brackets.
- The items in brackets are information passed to the procedure, this is covered in later chapters.
- The **Handles** keyword is used to specify the name of the control and the event which this procedure handles.

- The words **End Sub** marks the end of the event handler.

We need the following code within the event handler to display the open dialog.

```
OpnImageFile.Filter = "Windows bitmap files(*.bmp)|*.bmp"
OpnImageFile.InitialDirectory( ) = CurDir("C")
OpnImageFile.ShowDialog( )
picHoliday.Image = System.Drawing.Image.FromFile(OpnImageFile.FileName)
btnBigger.Enabled = True
btnSmaller.Enabled = True
```

At this stage the code window should be similar to Figure 4.4.

```
FrmShrinkingAndGrowing (WindowsApplication1)          btnOpenFile_Click

    Private Sub btnOpenFile_Click(ByVal eventSender As System.Object, _
    ByVal eventArgs As System.EventArgs) Handles btnOpenFile.Click
        OpnImageFile.Filter = "Windows bitmap files(*.bmp)|*.bmp"
        OpnImageFile.InitialDirectory() = CurDir("C")
        OpnImageFile.ShowDialog()
        picHoliday.Image = System.Drawing.Image.FromFile(OpnImageFile.FileN
        btnBigger.Enabled = True
        btnSmaller.Enabled = True
    End Sub
```

Figure 4.4 *The Button **Click** event procedure.*

One of the excellent aspects of Visual Basic is that you can run your application at any stage in its development. If you run the application at this point and click on the top button the open dialog will appear as shown in Figure 4.5, showing initially the top level directory on the C: disk.

- The **Filter** property ensures that only files with a .bmp extension are displayed.
- The **InitialDirectory** property gives the initial directory which the open dialog displays.
- The **ShowDialog** method displays the dialog.
- The file you select from the dialog is returned as *OpnImageFile*.**FileName**. This is assigned to the **Image** property of the **PictureBox** control using the **System.Drawing.Image.FromFile** method.

- The **Enabled** property of the remaining two buttons which change the size of the picture are assigned to **True**, so that they are made available for use.

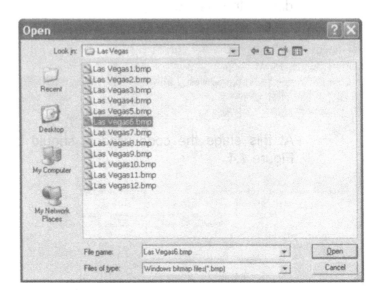

Figure 4.5 Opening a file.

To make the buttons change the size of the image we need to add some code to the event procedures for the remaining two **Button** controls.

The Button event handlers

We need to add event handlers for the **Button** controls, so that when one is selected, the required action is taken.

To create the template event procedure:

- Select *btnBigger* from the list of controls in the left menu on the code window.
- Select **Click** from the list of events in the right menu.

The outline event procedure is shown below:

```
Private Sub btnBigger_Click(ByVal eventSender As System.Object, _
   ByVal eventArgs As System.EventArgs) Handles btnBigger.Click

End Sub
```

This is exactly the same format as for the **OpenFileDialog** event handler: the name of the procedure comprises the name of the control, an underscore and the name of the event. To make the picture 10% bigger in this event procedure we must increase the **Height** and **Width** properties of the **PictureBox** control. We do this by multiplying them by 1.1. The event procedure becomes:

```
Private Sub btnBigger_Click(ByVal eventSender As System.Object, _
   ByVal eventArgs As System.EventArgs) Handles btnBigger.Click
      picHoliday.Width = picHoliday.Width * 1.1
      picHoliday.Height = picHoliday.Height * 1.1
   End Sub
```

Similarly the event procedure for the remaining button which makes the images smaller is:

```
Private Sub btnSmaller_Click(ByVal eventSender As System.Object, _
   ByVal eventArgs As System.EventArgs) Handles btnSmaller.Click
      picHoliday.Width = picHoliday.Width / 1.1
      picHoliday.Height = picHoliday.Height / 1.1
   End Sub
```

Note that the **Size.Height** and the **Size.Width** properties cannot be used to change the height and width, they can only be used to report their value. the **Width** and **Size** properties must be used instead.

If you want to try this application for yourself you will need to use your own pictures (or download this application from the series web site www.Essential-series.com) and to specify their full path name.

A quick way of making event procedures

There is a short cut to making the most common event handlers, rather than displaying the code window and selecting the control and the type of event procedure you want. All you have to do to create the most common event procedure for a control is to double click on that control on the design form. This automatically opens the code window, creates the event procedure and positions the cursor in the correct position for you to add your Visual Basic code.

The event procedure, created by this method, for **Button**, **RadioButton** and **CheckBox** controls is the **Click** event, for forms it is the **Load** event. Note that empty event procedures are not automatically deleted when the application is run, as in previous versions of Visual Basic.

The IntelliSense facility

If you have tried the last application for yourself you will have noticed some menus popping up when you were typing, these are a part of the IntelliSense facility. When you start to enter your code, Visual Basic provides hints or tips which help you to write syntactically correct code. There are six types of assistance provided:

- List Members.
- Parameter Information.
- Quick Information.
- Complete Word.
- Automatic Brace Matching.
- Visual Basic-Specific IntelliSense.

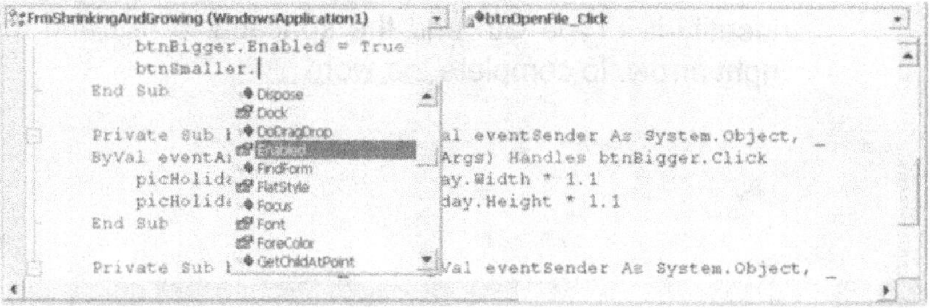

Figure 4.6 *The List Members facility.*

The List Members facility can be seen when you type the name of any object. The properties of that object are listed, as shown in Figure 4.6.

The Parameter Information facility indicates available parameters, for example, in Figure 4.7 the **CurDir** function has two possible sets of parameters, the second one is a single character which specifies the disk drive.

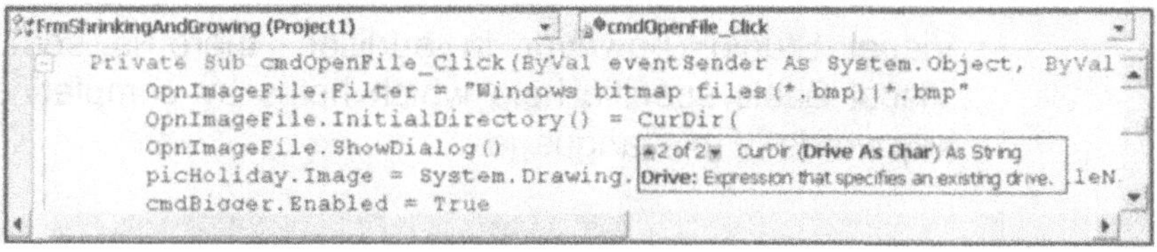

Figure 4.7 *The Parameter Information facility.*

When you are intending to assign the property of an object, a list of possible values is displayed as shown in Figure 4.8. If you wish to insert one of the possible options into your code, click on that option, or move to it by using the arrowed keys and press the **Tab** key.

The Quick Information facility gives complete details of the declaration of any identifier. This is displayed when the mouse rests on an identifier.

The Complete Word facility provides the remainder of a word when sufficient characters have been typed to identify it. Type Ctrl and the spacebar or Alt and the right arrow, to complete the word.

```
FrmShrinkingAndGrowing (WindowsApplication1)        btnOpenFile_Click
        btnBigger.Enabled = True
        btnSmaller.Enabled =
    End Sub                          False
                                     True
    Private Sub btnBigger_Click(ByVal eventSender As System.Object, _
    ByVal eventArgs As System.EventArgs) Handles btnBigger.Click
        picHoliday.Width = picHoliday.Width * 1.1
        picHoliday.Height = picHoliday.Height * 1.1
    End Sub

    Private Sub btnSmaller_Click(ByVal eventSender As System.Object,
```

Figure 4.8 *Displaying acceptable values.*

One of the most common mistakes in programming is to have brackets which do not match. The Automatic Brace Matching facility ensures that a brace remains highlighted until a matching brace of the opposite sort is typed.

These facilities are available to the other members of Visual Studio, however in addition, there is some Visual Basic specific help which helps by completing key words of this language.

Chapter 5

Variables and Operators

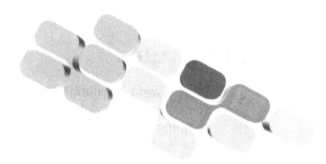

Introduction

In most programming languages when we want to represent a piece of data within an application we need to decide what type it is. For example, the number of people working in a company is likely to be a whole number, that is an Integer data type; your name can be represented by a series of characters, that is a String data type, and so on. Visual Basic is one of the few languages which allow you to use variables without first declaring what type they are. Visual Basic does offer you the option of declaring the type of variables before using them, and there are some important benefits to doing this. The type of a variable determines what operations you can carry out on it, for example you cannot multiply a text string.

In this chapter we are going to look at :

- Naming rules and conventions
- The Visual Basic data types.

Naming rules

If you want to change the name of controls from their default or you want to name variables, there are some naming rules which you must follow. In addition there are some conventions which are followed by most Visual Basic programmers and constitute good practice. Variable names must conform to these rules:

- Must begin with a letter.
- Must not contain an embedded period of one of the type declaration characters (for example $).
- Must be unique within its scope.

The length of names is for all practical purposes unlimited.

Naming controls

When you create a control, Visual Basic will assign it a default name, but it is important to rename each object appropriately. It helps to make the code more readable if you allocate a prefix to each type of control object, for example *frm* for a form. An appropriate name for your initial splash screen would be *frmSplash*, which is far more meaningful than the default *Form1*.

Some suggested prefixes for common controls are shown in Table 5.1.

Table 5.1 Suggested prefixes for controls.

Control	Prefix	Example
CheckBox	chk	chkInterlaced
ComboBox	cbo	cboDestination
Button	btn	btnOK
Form	frm	frmExit
Label	lbl	lblAddress
ListBox	lst	lstAirport
Menu	mnu	mnuHelp
PictureBox	pic	picHetty
RichTextBox	rtb	rtbDetails
Text box	txt	txtHotelDetails
Timer	tim	timCountdown

Adding comments

Another important aspect of making your applications easy to read and understand is to add comments. This is text which is added simply for the programmers benefit – it has no impact on how that application runs. To add a comment, use the ' character. The remainder of the line will be ignored by Visual Basic and you can type whatever text you wish.

```
'this is a line of comment
    picHoliday.Width = picHoliday.Width * 1.1          'this is also comment
```

If you want to have more than one line of comments you must add the comment symbol at the start of every line.

For backward compatibility with very early versions of Visual Basic you may also use the reserved word **REM** in place of the ' character.

Variable types

Visual Basic offers an extensive range of twelve data types as shown in Table 5.2.

Table 5.2 Data types.

Type	Size in bytes	Suffix
Boolean	2	No suffix.
Byte	1	No suffix.
Char	2	No suffix.
Date	8	No suffix.
Decimal	16	@
Double	8	#
Integer	4	%
Long	8	&
Object	4	No suffix.
Short	2	None
Single	4	!
String	Dependent on string size.	$

There are two ways of defining the type of a variable explicitly using the **Dim** statement or one of its variants (as described in detail later in this chapter):

```
Dim intAge as Integer
Dim intAge%
```

The two forms shown above both define an **Integer** variable. The second form indicates the type by the %

suffix. Similarly, *strMyLine$* is a **String** and *lng&* is a variable of type **Long**. It is good programming practice to declare variables before they are used, and to use the naming conventions we are going to look at next. The use of suffixes to indicate the variable type is becoming less popular among professional programmers.

Naming conventions for variables

We have looked at the naming conventions for control objects, in a similar way there are a set of conventions for the different variable data types.

Table 5.3 Suggested prefixes for variables.

Type	Prefix	Example
Boolean	bln	blnMale
Byte	byt	bytAge
Char	chr	chrInitial
Decimal	dec	decGDPTurkey
Double	dbl	dblAverage
Integer	int	intPeopleInRoom
Long	lng	lngResult
Object	obj	objNew
Short	sht	shtPCCost
Single	sng	sngHeight
String	str	strAddress

It is often very helpful to be able to determine at a glance what type a variable is, without checking to see what it has been declared as. Table 5.3 lists some suggested prefixes which are widely used for the different data types.

Naming conventions

While you must adhere to the naming rules for your application to run, it is good practice to follow some standard naming conventions. These are just a set of rules that Visual Basic programmers have agreed to follow to make their programs readable and easier to understand.

Choosing meaningful names

Some old programming languages and operating systems limited the number of characters you could use in a variable name. These limitations do not apply in Visual Basic, names can be as long as you want, so use complete words rather than abbreviations. Names up to about 15 characters are the best length. Some examples are given in Table 5.4.

Table 5.4 Choosing appropriate variable names.

Good	Poor
intTotal	Tot
shtTotalWeight	TotWt
strMrsHettyWaintrop	Mrs_Hetty_Wainthrop
sngAverageMayTemperature	TheAverageOfAllTheTemperaturesInMay

If a name comprises more than one word, separate the words by using a capital letter at the start of the word as shown in Table 5.4. It is no longer common practice to use underscores to separate words.

Choosing consistent names

Problems are caused by incorrectly spelt names, for example, *aplication* rather than *application*. If another person has to make changes to your program it can take quite a while to spot misspellings.

Another problem, particularly when more than one person is writing a large application is to change the word order. For example, if you are recording information about a window it is a good idea to agree that the word *Window* will always come first, so that names such as *WindowSize*, *WindowPosition*, and *WindowColour* are used rather than using the first two names and then *ColourWindow* in place of the third.

Declaring variables

One of the most common mistakes in Visual Basic is to misspell the name of a variable. This does not cause a syntax error, but the program does not behave as expected. One way around this is to declare the name and type of variables prior to their first use; the **Dim** statement is one way of doing this, for example:

```
Dim intAge As Integer, sngAverage As Single
```

This statement has many controls, however most of them are optional. The general form is:

```
[<attributeList>] Dim [WithEvents] name [<boundlist> ] [As [New] type] [=initexpr]
```

All the items in [ ] brackets are optional.

The attribute list is a set of optional parameters which can be any of the following, if you want multiple parameters they are separated by commas. The attributes are:

Public. There are no restrictions on where **Public** variables can be accessed, however a variable can only be declared **Public** inside a module, class or structure not inside a procedure.

Protected. A **Protected** variable is only accessible from within its own class or a sub class. A **Protected** variable may only be declared within a class, not within a procedure.

Friend. A **Friend** variable is accessible from within the program. **Friend** variables can only be declared from within a module, class or structure, not within a procedure.

Protected Friend. The access is the union of the access and restrictions provided by both **Protected** and **Friend**.

Private. A **Private** variable is accessible from within the file, module, class or structure where it is defined. It cannot be declared within a procedure.

Static. A **Static** variable is not destroyed after the procedure in which it is declared ends. Static variables may only be declared in procedures.

Shared. A **Shared** variable is not associated with any particular instance of a class or structure. **Shared** variables may be declared in a file, module, class or structure, but not inside a procedure.

Shadows. The variable shadows an identically named variable which has already been declared. May be used in a file, module, class or structure but not inside a procedure.

ReadOnly. The value of a **ReadOnly** variable cannot be changed. **ReadOnly** variables may be declared in a file, module, class or structure, but not inside a procedure.

If you have used none of these attributes the **Dim** keyword comes next, if you have one or more it may be omitted. If you do type it, Visual Basic automatically removes it for you.

The optional **WithEvents** keyword specifies that the name which follows is an object variable used to respond to events.

The *name* is a mandatory parameter which is a valid identifier name. You can specify more than one name separated by commas.

The *boundlist* is an optional parameter which lists the upper bounds of all of the dimensions of an array which is being declared. Each of the integer values are separated by commas.

The optional **New** keyword is used to instantiate or create an object.

The **As** keyword is followed by a valid Visual Basic data type. If no type is specified the variable takes on the type of **Object**.

The *initexpr* is an optional parameter which assigns an initial value to a variable. If the type is not specified the variable takes on the type indicated by the initial value specified.

The **Dim** statement has grown from simple beginnings to be one of the most complex statements in the language. To understand how it is used in practice a few examples are shown below:

```
Private intAge As Integer = 73, strSurname As String
Public dblCost As Double, dblInvest As Double = 17.5
Dim strFirstName As String = "Hetty"
Dim strSurname$ = "Wainthrop"          'The $ makes it implicitly a String
```

Option Explicit statement

It is a good idea to make variable declaration mandatory by either:

- Forcing explicit declarations in each module, by putting the statement **Option Explicit On** at the start of the modules before any procedures.
- If you wish to make variable declaration a requirement for the whole project click on the project name (not the solution name), then click on the Properties button, as shown in Figure 5.1, to display the Properties Dialog.

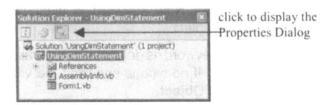

click to display the Properties Dialog

Figure 5.1 *Displaying the Properties Dialog.*

In the Properties Dialog click on **Build** in the left **TextBox** to display the page shown in Figure 5.2.

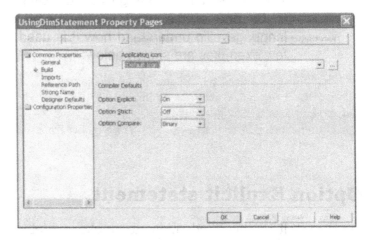

Figure 5.2 *The Properties Dialog.*

Turn **Option Explicit** to **On** in this dialog. You can override this for a specific module by using the statement **Option Explicit Off** at its start.

Option Strict statement

The **Option Strict** statement is a companion to the **Option Explicit** statement and can be used in the same way, both at the project and module level. If you use **Option Strict**, **Option Explicit** is automatically turned on.

In Visual Basic if two variables of different types are assigned to each other, there is an implicit conversion from one type to another. Data types can be thought of as weak or strong, the greater the range of values a type can represent the stronger it is. For example, **Integer** is a stronger type than **Byte**. A stronger type can always store a value saved in a weaker type, although there may be a loss of accuracy if, for example, an **Integer** is assigned to a floating point type such as **Single**. If **Option Strict** is turned on, an error message is displayed at compile time if an attempt is made to assign a stronger type to a weaker type.

Declaring constants

Sometimes you may want to use a value which will not change throughout the life of the application. Visual Basic makes extensive use of constants, for example, when providing a set of options for the property of a control. To define your own constant values, which cannot be changed, the **Const** keyword is used.

The **Const** statement is very similar to the **Dim** statement. Constants are defined throughout the class, module, structure or procedure in which they are defined. Two examples are shown below:

```
Const intMonthsInYear As Integer = 12
Const dblPi As Double = 3.142
```

The Boolean data type

The **Boolean** type is used for data which can have only one of two possible values, for example **True** / **False** or **Yes** / **No** type variables. Booleans can be assigned using the keywords **True** and **False**. For example:

```
blnBuy = False
```

Data types representing integers

There are four data types which are used for representing integers: **Byte**, **Short**, **Integer** and **Long**. The type you choose to use is dependent on the range of numbers you want to use. The greater the range of numbers which can be stored, the greater the space required by the variable.

You can make a variable an **Integer** by placing the % character at the end of its name. You can declare a **Long** using the & character in the same way, for example:

```
intDaysInJanuary% = 31                ' an Integer
lngGDPTurkey& = 7540000000000  ' GDP of turkey (>1,500,000 to the dollar)
```

Data types representing floating point numbers

There are three data types which can represent floating point numbers: **Single, Double** and **Decimal**.

The single floating point type should be used where accuracy is not paramount. Operations are still relatively quick on this type, although much slower than on the integer types. The suffix indicating a **Single** value is !, for a **Double** the character is #, for example:

```
sngAverageTemperatureOfHawaii! = 27.3      ' Single value (in centigrade)
dblPi# = 3.141592                          ' Double value
```

The **Decimal** data type replaces the **Currency** data type which is no longer supported. The **Decimal** type stores numbers as 16 byte signed integers multiplied by a power of ten which may vary from 0 to 28. This type should be used to store money values. The suffix for the **Decimal** type is @.

```
decBillGatesIncome@ = 2345674635
```

If you wish to assign a large literal to a **Decimal** you should append the letter D after the literal, for example:

```
decAtomsInUniverse@ = 3416000000000D
```

The Date data type

The **Date** type does not have a suffix, but when assigning a date to a variable of this type, the date, and time if you wish, is enclosed between two # characters, for example:

```
Dim dtmChristmasDay As Date, dtmSomeDay As Date
dtmChristmasDay = #12/25/2001#
dtmSomeDay = #7/15/2003 2:20:00 PM#
```

The date must follow the format mm/dd/yyyy

```
Dim dtmChristmasEve as Date
dtmChristmasDay = dtmChristmasEve + 1
```

A useful function is **Now** which returns the current date and time, for example:

```
Dim dtmTodaysDateAndTime as Date
dtmTodaysDateandTime = Now
```

The Object data type

The **Object** type is used to address an object. A variable of this type may be assigned to an instance of a class or any other data type.

The String data type

This data type is used to contain a sequence of characters. The Unicode character set is used. You can concatenate strings using the & operator, for example:

```
Dim strFirstPerson As String, strSecondPerson As String
Dim strMessage As String
strFirstPerson = "Daisy"
strSecondPerson = "Lily"
strMessage = strFirstPerson & " and " & strSecondPerson & " are lazy and silly"
```

You can also use the + operator to concatenate strings, but this can cause some problems where the strings to be concatenated could be converted to numeric values, for example:

```
Dim txtAdd as String, txtConcatenate as String
txtAdd=7 + 8
txtConcatenate = 7 & 8
```

The string *txtAdd* will display 15, the result of adding 7 and 8, while *txtConcatenate* will display 78, the result of concatenating the two strings.

You can use the type identifier character, $, to indicate that a variable is a **String**, or use a **Dim** statement to declare it.

The Char data type

The **Char** data type is used to represent a single character. You can force a literal to be of **Char** data type by adding the letter c after it, for example:

```
Dim chrInitial as Char
chrInitial = "J"c
```

If the **Option Strict On** statement is not in force for this procedure, Visual Basic will automatically convert the single character **String** "J" into a **Char** data type anyway.

The range of data types

The different data types can represent different ranges of values with different accuracies, depending on the format and the number of bytes used. The range of these types is shown in Table 5.5.

Table 5.5 The range of data types.

Type	Most Negative	Most Positive
Boolean	Not applicable.	Not applicable.
Byte	0	255
Char	Not applicable.	Not applicable.
Date	Earliest : January 1 0001.	Latest : December 31 9999.
Decimal	-79,228,162,414,264,337,593, 543,950,335	79,228,162,414,264,337,593, 543,950,335
Double	-1.797 693 134 862 32 E308	1.797 693 134 862 32 E308
Integer	-2,147,483,648	2,147,483,647
Long	-9,223,372,036,854,775,808	9,223,372,036,854,775,807
Object	Not applicable.	Not applicable.
Short	-32,768	32,767
Single	-3.402 823 5 E38	3.402 823 5 E38
String	Not applicable.	Approx. 65,400 characters.

Converting between data types

Sometimes you may need to convert from one data type to another, Visual Basic provides a comprehensive set of functions which allow you to do this as listed in Table 5.6.

When converting from a floating point to an integer the number is always rounded to the nearest value.

Table 5.6 Functions for converting between data types.

Function	Return type	Function	Return type
CBool	Boolean	CInt	Integer
CByte	Byte	CLng	Long
CChar	Character	CObj	Object
CDate	Date	CSng	Single
CDbl	Double	CShort	Short
CDec	Decimal	CStr	String

To see a few of these functions in action we are going to look at a simple application, shown running in Figure 5.3. The two numbers typed into the **TextBox** controls are averaged and when the **Button** control is pressed, the result displayed in a **Label** control.

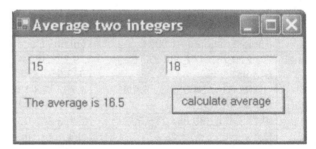

Figure 5.3 *Averaging two integers.*

The code for this event is contained in the event handler for the **Button** control.

```
Private Sub btnCalculate_Click(ByVal sender As System.Object, _
    ByVal e As System.EventArgs) Handles btnCalculate.Click
        Dim intTotal As Integer
        Dim sngAverage As Single
        intTotal = CInt(TextBox1.Text) + CInt(TextBox2.Text)
        sngAverage = CSng(intTotal) / 2
        LblResult.Text = "The average is " & CStr(sngAverage)
End Sub
```

The values typed into the **TextBox** controls are of type **String** and are stored in the **Text** property of those controls. These values are converted into **Integer** using the **CInt** function and added to give the **Integer** variable *intTotal*. This is converted into a floating point type, **Single**, using the **CSng** function divided by two and the result assigned to the *sngAverage* **Single** variable. The result is displayed in the **Text** property of the **Label**, but must be converted from **Single** to **String** using the **CStr** function.

Arithmetic operators

We have looked at a few of the operators which Visual Basic uses for arithmetic. The complete list is shown in Table 5.7.

Table 5.7 The arithmetic operators.

Operator	Action	Example
+	Addition.	3 + 7 = 11
-	Subtraction.	8 - 2 = 6
*	Multiplication.	2.1 * 4 = 8.4
/	Division.	20.2 / 2 = 10.1
^	Exponentiation.	3 ^ 2 = 9
\	Integer division.	6 \ 5 = 1
Mod	Modulus, returns the remainder after integer division.	8 **Mod** 3 = 2

Assignment operators

We have already seen the basic assignment operator =, but there are another seven which are shorthand ways of carrying out mathematical operations as well as performing an assignment, for example:

```
Dim intA as Integer = 2
Dim intB as Integer = 3
intA *= intB                'intA = 6, intB unchanged
```

The statement:

```
intA *= intB
```

has the same effect as:

```
intA = intA * intB
```

The full set of operators are shown in Table 5.8:

Table 5.8 The assignment operators.

Operator	Example	Meaning
+=	intA += 2	intA = intA + 2
-=	intA -= 2	intA = intA - 2
*=	intA *= 2	intA = intA * 2
/=	intA /= 2	intA = intA / 2
^=	intA ^= 2	intA = intA ^ 2
\=	intA \= 2	intA = intA \ 2
&=	strA &= strB	strA = strA & strB

Note that the &= operator is used to concatenate two **String** variables.

Arrays

Arrays are used to collect together pieces of data which are of the same type: for example a list of people's names could be stored as an array of type **String**, a list of exam marks could be stored as an array of type **Integer**. Arrays can have more than one dimension, for example a timetable could be stored as a two–dimensional array. Up to sixty dimensions are allowed.

Declaring arrays

Before an array can be used it must be declared using the **Dim** statement.

```
Dim name (subscripts) [As type]
```

The simplest arrays have only one dimension, for example:

```
Dim strNameList(5) As String
```

> This defines a one–dimensional array with six elements: *strNameList(0)* to *strNameList(5)*. The lower bound is always zero in Visual Basic .NET. These elements can be used anywhere a variable of their type could be used, for example:

```
strNameList(0) = "John Cowell"
```

Changing array dimensions

> You can declare an array without specifying its size, for example:

```
Dim intRange( ) As Integer      ' declare an array
```

> The size can be specified with a **ReDim** statement:

```
ReDim intRange(300)             ' specify the dimensions of the declared array
```

> In addition you can change the size of an existing array with the **ReDim** statement. When you do so all the information in the array is lost unless the **Preserve** keyword is used, for example:

> You can use the **ReDim** statement repeatedly to change the size of the array at run–time.

```
Dim Range( ) As Integer            'declare an integer array
ReDim intRange (20)             ' declare its size
ReDim Preserve intRange (30)       'change its size retaining all data.
```

> The advantage of the **ReDim** statement is that by decreasing the array size at some point in a program where a large array is no longer required you can free memory. If you wish to free all the memory an array is using, the **Erase** statement can be used, for example:

```
Erase intArray
```

Structures

Visual Basic allows you to group related pieces of data together: for example if you want to save information on a collection of computers in an office, including the processor type, the memory size and cost, you can create a data type which groups this information together and then define an array of this type. The information we want to save is shown in Table 5.9. Each row represents our new data type.

Table 5.9 User–defined data types.

Processor	Memory Size	Cost
Pentium 4 2.1GHz	512	200.00
Pentium 3 1.5 GHz	256	110.00
Pentium 3 1.2 GHz	128	60.00

The **Structure..End Structure** construct is used to define the data type. The structure shown below is called *Computer* and contains three different elements.

```
Structure Computer
    Public strProcessor As String
    Public shtMemorySize As Short
    Public sglCost As Single
End Structure
```

Variables can be defined to be of the structure defined, or even arrays as shown below:

```
Dim CompanyPC(2) As Computer
CompanyPC(0).strProcessor = "Pentium 4 2.0GHz"
CompanyPC(0).shtMemorySize = 512
CompanyPC(0).sglCost = 200.00
```

This code creates an array called *CompanyPC* with 3 elements each of which has its own *strProcessor*, *shtMemorySize* and *sglCost* variables.

The **Structure** construct can only be declared in a source file, a module or a class, but not inside a procedure.

Chapter

6

Controlling Program Flow

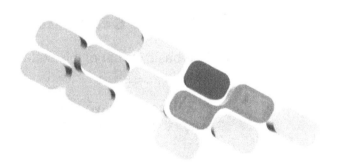

Introduction

One of the key features of Visual Basic, in common with other programming languages is the ability to make decisions on the basis of information. For example, if you are writing an application for calculating the cost of car insurance and a person gives his age as 18, the premiums will be higher than for an older person: the application calculates a different cost depending on age. In Chapter four we saw how to respond to the events which occur when an application runs, but we did not see how to take these sorts of decisions, that is how to control the program flow.

In this chapter we are going to look at:

- Constructs for making decisions.
- Looping constructs.

The If..Then statement

The basic format of this statement is:

```
If condition Then statement
```

If you want to have more than one statement executed when the **If** condition is met, the format is:

```
If condition Then
    statement
    statement
    .....
End If
```

The **If** condition takes the form of a comparison between two values, for example a test for equality or to see if one value is greater or less than another.

We are going to look at an application which uses **If Then** statements. The running application is shown in Figure 6.1.

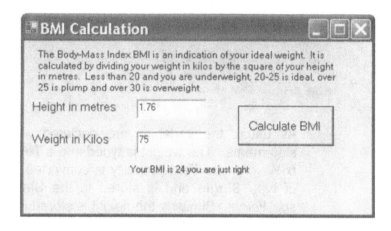

Figure 6.1 *Calculating Body-Mass Index.*

This application calculates the BMI, Body-Mass Index, which is an indication of whether a person is overweight, underweight or about right. The BMI is calculated by dividing the weight in kilos by the square of the height in metres. A BMI of between 20 and 25 is regarded as ideal, less than this indicates underweight and different degrees of overweight.

The application has two **TextBox** controls where the height and weight are entered. These are named *txtHeight* and *txtWeight*. The **Button** control is called *btnCalculate*. The **Label** at the bottom of the form where the result is displayed is called *lblResult*. The text at the top of the form and alongside the **TextBox** is displayed using three more **Label** controls.

The event procedure for the **Button** is shown below:

```
Private Sub btnCalculate_Click(ByVal eventSender As System.Object, _
ByVal eventArgs As System.EventArgs) Handles btnCalculate.Click
    Dim sngWeight As Single, sngHeight As Single
    Dim intBmi As Integer
    Dim strM As String
```

```
    sngWeight = CSng(txtWeight.Text)  ' convert to single
    sngHeight = CSng(txtHeight.Text)
    intBmi = CInt(sngWeight / sngHeight ^ 2) 'convert result to integer
    strM = "Your BMI is " & CStr(intBmi) & " you are "
    If intBmi < 20 Then strM = strM & "underweight"
    If intBmi >= 20 And intBmi <= 25 Then strM = strM & "just right"
    If intBmi > 25 And intBmi <= 30 Then strM = strM & "plump"
    If intBmi > 30 Then strM = strM & "overweight"
    lblResult.Text = strM
End Sub
```

As usual, the variables are declared with the **Dim** statements. The weight is typed into a **TextBox** called *txtWeight*. Its **Text** property is converted into a value of type **Single** and is stored in the **Single** variable *sngWeight*. Similarly the height is stored in *sngHeight*. The BMI is then calculated. The first part of the message which is displayed is stored in the **String** *strM*. Checks are made using the **If..Then** statement and some text added to the **String** *strM*. Finally the message is displayed in the **Label** called *lblResult* using its **Text** property.

The If..Then..Else statement

The repeated **If..Then** statements in the last application can be improved can be improved by using **If..Then..Else** statements. The basic format of this statement is :

```
If condition1 Then
        statement
        statement
        .....
ElseIf condition2 Then
        statement
        statement
        .....
Else
        statement
```

```
          statement
          ......
End If
```

You can add as many **Else** clauses as you wish, however many you add, a maximum of one of them is executed. If none of the **If** conditions are met, none of the statements are executed. This part of our application now becomes:

```
If intBmi < 20 Then
        strM = strM & "underweight"
Elself intBmi <= 25 Then
        strM = strM & "just right"
Elself intBmi <= 30 Then
        strM = strM & "plump"
Else
        strM = strM & "overweight"
End If
```

The functionality is exactly the same, but this will execute faster than the previous form. In addition, the statement is easier to read and the conditions which are tested are simpler. If the first part of the statement which displays the message *underweight* is displayed *intBmi* is less than 20. If this condition is not met and it proceeds to the next part of the statement we know that *intBmi* is 20 or greater and therefore only need to test to see if it is less or equal to than 25, and so on.

Using the Select Case statement

The **Select Case** statement is a useful alternative to using **If..Then..Else** statements, it is often easier to read. The basic form of this statement is:

```
Select Case test expression
    Case expression list1
            statements
    Case expression list2
            statements

    ......
```

```
Case Else
        statements
End Select
```

There are a number of restrictions on how **Select Case** statements can be used; the test expression must be one of the following:

- A literal or expression which evaluates to one of the following types: **Boolean**, **Byte**, **Char**, **Date**, **Double**, **Decimal**, **Integer**, **Long**, **Object**, **Short**, **Single**, or **String**.
- A range using the keyword **To**.
- A conditional range using the keyword **Is**.

The use of the keyword **Is** shown below. The code below is functionally the same as the code in our previous two forms of the BMI application.

```
Select Case intBmi
        Case Is < 20
                strM = strM & "underweight"
        Case Is <= 25
                strM = strM & "just right"
        Case Is <= 30
                strM = strM & "plump"
        Case Else
                strM = strM & "overweight"
End Select
```

An example of using the **To** statement is shown below:

```
Case 20 To 25
```

You can also specify more than one value, for example:

```
Case 20,21,22,23,24
```

The comparison operators

We have already seen two comparison operators, the < operator which means *less than* and the <= operator which means *less than* or *equal to*. The full set of comparison operators is shown in Table 6.1:

Table 6.1 The comparison operators.

Operator	Action
=	Equal.
<	Less than.
>	Greater than.
<=	Less than or equal.
>=	Greater than or equal.
<>	Not equal.

These operators can be used on strings as well as numeric values.

Looping

Some of the most common programming structures in Visual Basic are the looping constructs: these allow you to repeat a block of code many times, perhaps changing the value of a variable each time. There are four types of construct:

- **For...Next**
- **For Each...Next**
- **While**
- **Do...Loop**

The For..Next statement

It is quite common to increase or decrease a counter within a loop and Visual Basic provides a statement which does this. The general form of the **For**..**Next** loop is:

```
For counter = start To end Step value
        statements                 ' as many statements as you wish
        Exit For                   ' this optional statement exits from the loop
        statements                 ' as many statements as you wish
Next                               ' increase the counter and go to start of loop
```

The counter is a numerical value (usually **Integer**) which is assigned the start value the first time the loop is executed. The loop continues until the counter has reached the end value. If you wish you can specify the reserved word **Step** and a value. Every time the loop is executed the counter has this value added to it. The step value can be positive or negative. If you omit the **Step** reserved word and its value, the counter is increased by one every time the loop is executed. Loops operate faster when the counter is an **Integer** rather than any other data type.

We are going to look at a small application which uses a **For**..**Next** loop and also how you can add some error trapping to an application, so that when an error occurs the application does not crash. The running application is shown in Figure 6.2.

The application calculates how many rabbits there will be from an initial population after a specified number of years. Some pretty unreliable assumptions are made in this application, it assumes that: there are equal numbers of male and female rabbits; four rabbits are born per litter; two litters are born per year; newly born rabbits are ready to breed at the same time as their parents; rabbits never die.

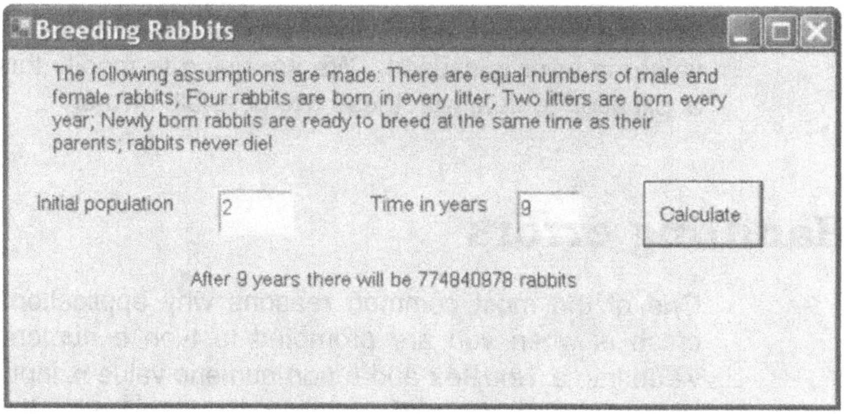

Figure 6.2 *Calculating the number of rabbits.*

The unreliable assumptions explain why the entire planet is not overrun with rabbits. The code for this application, shown below, is entirely in the event procedure for the **Click** event of the button.

```
Private Sub btnCalculate_Click(ByVal eventSender As System.Object, _
ByVal eventArgs As System.EventArgs) Handles btnCalculate.Click
    Dim shtTimeInYears As Short
    Dim shtInitialNumber As Short
    Dim intFinalNumber As Integer
    Const shtNumberPerLitter As Short = 4
    Dim c As Short
    shtTimeInYears = CShort(txtTimeInYears.Text)
    shtInitialNumber = CInt(txtInitialNumber.Text)
    intFinalNumber = shtInitialNumber
'two breeding cycles per year and 4 rabbits per litter
    For c = 1 To shtTimeInYears * 2
        intFinalNumber = intFinalNumber + intFinalNumber / 2 * _
            shtNumberPerLitter
    Next c
    lblResult.Text = "After " & txtTimeInYears.Text & " years there will be " _
            & CStr(intFinalNumber) & " rabbits"
End Sub
```

The application works well but can be made to crash easily. If you input a non-numeric value in either of the **TextBox** controls or if the number of rabbits is greater than the maximum value which can be stored in a long value an error is caused. We are going to modify this application to deal with these two possible errors.

Handling errors

One of the most common reasons why applications crash is when you are prompted to type a numeric value into a **TextBox** and a non-numeric value is input instead. One way of handling this is to use the **IsNumeric** function, which returns a **True** value if the expression it is given can be converted to a numeric value and **False** if it cannot, for example:

```
If IsNumeric(txtTimeInYears.Text) Then
    shtTimeInYears = CShort(txtTimeInYears.Text)
    Else : Exit Sub
End If
```

If the value input to the **TextBox** called *txtTimeInYears* is numeric then the **CShort** function is used to actually carry out the conversion. If it is not, the procedure is exited. If you wish you can take further action such as displaying a warning message.

The On Error Statement

Another technique for trapping errors is to use the **On Error** statement. When an error occurs, program control is transferred to an error handling routine. There are four forms of this statement:

```
On Error GoTo line
```

Transfers control to a line number or line label.

```
On Error Resume Next
```

Transfers control to the line following the line where the error occurred.

On Error GoTo 0

> This statement disables any error handling in the current procedure.

On Error GoTo -1

> Disables an exception in the current procedure.

> The **On Error** statement has been added to our rabbit breeding application so that if the number of rabbits exceeds the maximum number which can stored in an **Integer** variable a message is displayed saying that there will be more than 2,147,483,647. The updated application is shown below:

```
Private Sub btnCalculate_Click(ByVal eventSender As System.Object, _
   ByVal eventArgs As System.EventArgs) Handles btnCalculate.Click
      Dim shtTimeInYears As Short
      Dim shtInitialNumber As Short
      Dim intFinalNumber As Integer
      Const shtNumberPerLitter As Short = 4
      Dim c As Short
      If IsNumeric(txtTimeInYears.Text) Then
          shtTimeInYears = CShort(txtTimeInYears.Text)
      Else : Exit Sub
      End If
      If IsNumeric(txtInitialNumber.Text) Then
              shtInitialNumber = CInt(txtInitialNumber.Text)
      Else : Exit Sub
      End If
      intFinalNumber = shtInitialNumber
'two breeding cycles per year and 4 rabbits per litter
      On Error GoTo ErrorHandler
      For c = 1 To shtTimeInYears * 2
          intFinalNumber = intFinalNumber + intFinalNumber / 2 * _
          shtNumberPerLitter
      Next c
      lblResult.Text = "After " & txtTimeInYears.Text & " years there will be " _
              & CStr(intFinalNumber) & " rabbits"
      Exit Sub
ErrorHandler:
      lblResult.Text = "After " & txtTimeInYears.Text & _
          " years there will be more than 2,147,483,647 rabbits"
End Sub
```

The error checking used here could be considerably extended to display warning messages or to clear incorrect fields. While the introduction of even simple error checking takes a lot of programming, it is crucial if your applications are to be resilient and not crash.

The For Each..Next statement

This statement is similar to the **For**..**Next** statement except that the loop is repeated for every element in a collection rather than a specified number of times. This is covered in Chapter 11 where an example of how it is used is given in the section on the **CheckBox** control.

The While statement

Another form of loop which does not have a loop counter built in is the **While** statement, this tests one or more conditions and executes a series of statements if they are met. The general form is:

```
While conditions
        statements      ' as many statements as you wish
        Exit While
        statements
End While
```

The **Exit While** statement leaves the loop. We are going to modify the previous application so that it will tell us how long before there are more than one million rabbits – using the same assumptions. The running application is shown in Figure 6.3.

The complete application is shown below:

```
Private Sub btnCalculate_Click(ByVal eventSender As System.Object, _
    ByVal eventArgs As System.EventArgs) Handles btnCalculate.Click
```

```
    Dim shtTimeInYears As Short
    Dim shtInitialNumber As Short
    Dim intFinalNumber As Integer
    Const shtNumberPerLitter As Short = 4
    If IsNumeric(txtInitialNumber.Text) Then
        shtInitialNumber = CInt(txtInitialNumber.Text)
    Else : Exit Sub
    End If
    intFinalNumber = shtInitialNumber
'two breeding cycles per year and 4 rabbits per litter
    shtTimeInYears = 0
    While intFinalNumber < 1000000
        intFinalNumber = intFinalNumber + intFinalNumber / 2 * _
            shtNumberPerLitter
        shtTimeInYears = shtTimeInYears + 1
' counting number of breeding cycles
    End While
' the rabbits breed twice per year so divide the number of years by 2
    shtTimeInYears = shtTimeInYears / 2
    lblResult.Text = "There will be more than 1,000,000 rabbits after " _
        & CStr(shtTimeInYears) & " Years"
End Sub
```

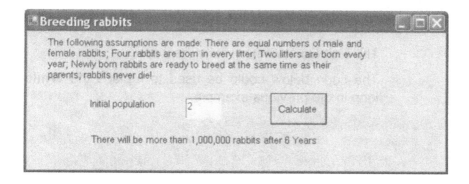

Figure 6.3 *How long to more than 1,000,000 rabbits?*

The test condition at the start of the **While** loop is to see if the variable *intFinalNumber* is less than one million, if this condition is not met (that is if the number is one million or more) the loop ends and the result is displayed. Every time the program loops the variable *intFinalNumber* is increased. This is the number of breeding cycles and is divided by two to give the number of years since the rabbits breed twice per year.

The Do..Loop statement

The **Do..Loop** statement is functionally very similar to the **While** statement.

There are two forms of this statement, the first tests one or more conditions at the start of the loop:

```
Do While conditions
      statements            ' as many statements as you wish
      Exit Do
      Statements
Loop
```

The alternative form tests at the end:

```
Do
      statements            ' as many statements as you wish
      Exit Do
      Statements
Loop While conditions
```

The **Exit Do** statement exits the loop.

The code below could be used to replace the **While** loop in the previous example.

```
Do While intFinalNumber < 1000000
      intFinalNumber = intFinalNumber + intFinalNumber / 2 *shtNumberPerLitter
      shtTimeInYears = shtTimeInYears + 1 ' number of breeding cycles
Loop
```

Functionally the application is the same as before.

You can reverse the form of this statement and place the test condition at the end:

```
Do
      intFinalNumber = intFinalNumber + intFinalNumber / 2 *shtNumberPerLitter
      shtTimeInYears = shtTimeInYears + 1
Loop Until intFinalNumber >= 1000000
```

In this application it is functionally the same, however this is not always the case. If the test condition is at the end of the loop, the loop will always execute at least one. If the test condition is at the start the loop may not be executed if that condition is not met.

Chapter 7

Functions and Procedures

Introduction

In a Windows environment whenever an event occurs a block of Visual Basic statements called an event handler is executed. An event handler is a procedure bound to an event. We have seen this in every application we have developed so far. In addition to using these procedures we can create our own. A procedure is just a collection of Visual Basic statements, in the case of event procedures they are linked to visual controls, while any other procedures we create are not. The advantage of creating new procedures rather than just writing all the Visual Basic code in event procedures is that a procedure may be called from more than one place, which reduces the need to duplicate code. Wherever possible it is best to reuse code as much as possible since it makes applications less complicated to test and reduces the number of possible errors. A function is very similar to a procedure except that it returns a value. In this chapter we are going to see how to create and use procedures and functions.

The Sub statement

Procedures start with the **Sub** statement and finish with the **End Sub** statement. The **Sub** statement is one of the most complex in Visual Basic with an extensive range of options, fortunately only a small subset of these tend to be commonly used. The form of these statements is:

```
[attributeList]Sub name [(argumentList)][Implements interface.definedname]
statements
[Exit Sub]
statements
End Sub
```

The **Exit Sub** statement is a way of exiting the procedure before the end of the procedure is reached as indicated by the **End Sub** statement.

The attributeList options

The attributeList is optional but may be one or more of the following attributes where they do not conflict. If more than one attribute is used, they are separated by commas.

The *attributeList* options are:

Overloads. Indicates that this procedure overrides one or more procedures of the same name in a base class.

Overrides. This procedure overrides a procedure of the same name and parameter list in the base class.

Overridable. This procedure may be overridden by a procedure of the same name and parameter list in the base class.

NotOverridable. This procedure cannot be overridden.

MustOverride. This procedure must be overridden in a derived class.

Shadows. This procedure shadows a procedure of the same name in a base class.

Shared. This procedure is not part of a specific object or structure. To call a shared procedure precede it with the class or structure name.

Public. There are no restrictions on access to this procedure.

Protected. This procedure is only accessible from its own class or from a derived class.

Friend. This procedure is accessible from anywhere within the application in which it is declared or from anywhere in the same assembly.

Protected Friend. Access is permitted by code in its own class, derived classes or anywhere in the same assembly.

Private. Access is permitted from within their declaration context, if for example a procedure is declared as **Private** within a class it may only be accessed in that class.

The argumentList options

The *argumentList* is an optional list of variables or expressions which is passed to the procedure. If included, the list must be enclosed in parentheses. Each list item has the following form:

```
[Optional] [ByVal | ByRef ] [ParamArray] argumentName [As argType]
[=defaultValue]
```

If more than one attribute is supplied they are separated by commas.

Optional. An optional parameter. The argument can be omitted. All following parameters must also be declared as **Optional**, in addition, a default value must be supplied.

ByVal. Optional. The argument is passed by value and if changed in the called procedure the change will not be reflected in the calling procedure. This is the default.

ByRef. Optional. The argument is passed by reference and if changed in the called procedure will also be changed in the calling procedure.

ParamArray. Optional. Used as the last argument to indicate that the final argument is an optional array of the specified type.

argumentName. Required. The name of the variable.

argType. The type of the variable. It can be either **Boolean**, **Byte**, **Char**, **Date**, **Decimal**, **Double**, **Integer**, **Long**, **Object**, **Short**, **Single**, **String**, or the name of an enumeration, structure, class or interface. The type must be preceded by the reserved word **As**. Optional unless **Option Strict** is **On**.

default. If a parameter is defined as **Optional** a default value must be supplied.

Two typical **Sub** statements are shown below:

```
Private Sub prime(ByRef intValue As Integer)
```

This procedure is **Private** and passed a single **Integer** parameter by reference.

```
Protected Friend Sub biggest(ByRef sngFirst As Single, Optional ByVal _
sngSecond As Single = 2.3)
```

The access of this procedure is **Protected Friend**, it has two **Single** parameters passed to it: the first by reference and the second by value. If the second optional parameter is not supplied a default value of 2.3 is used instead.

Although the **Sub** statement seems complex a small set of the options available are used for most applications.

The Password application

To see how procedures are used we are going to look at an application where a password is entered and checked to see if it is valid. If it is, a splash screen is displayed which in a full-scale application would provide a way into the application. If the password is incorrect, a warning dialog is displayed. Up to three attempts are allowed after which the application unloads the form and ends.

When the application is run, the form shown in Figure 7.1 is shown.

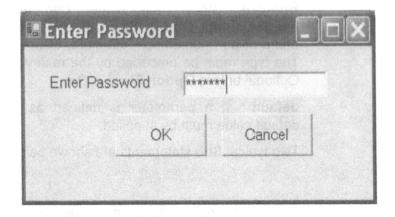

Figure 7.1 *The running password application.*

If an incorrect password is entered the message box on the left of Figure 7.2 is shown. If the correct password is entered the message on the right of Figure 7.2 is displayed.

Figure 7.2 *The application's message boxes.*

After entering the correct password and clicking on the **OK** button of the message box displayed, the splash screen shown in Figure 7.3 is shown.

Figure 7.3 *The splash screen indicating that the correct password has been entered.*

If the correct password is not entered after three attempts, or if the **Exit** button is clicked, another message box (shown in Figure 7.4) is displayed and the application ends.

Figure 7.4 *The failed logon dialog.*

To create this application:

- Change the name of the opening form to *frmPassword* and its **Text** property to *Enter password.*
- Change the name of the **TextBox** to *txtPassword* and set its **PasswordChar** property to *. This ensures that whatever is typed only this character appears. If you wish to limit the number of characters which can be entered you can do so with the **MaxLength** property.
- Add the **Label** which is alongside the **TextBox**.
- Change the name of the two buttons to *btnOk* and *btnCancel* and change the text they display.

- Add a splash screen to the application using the **Project | Add Windows Form** menu option and selecting the **Windows Forms** icon. Give this form the name *frmSplash*.

The code for the two **Click** event procedures for the two buttons is shown below. The **Show** method of displays a form, and the **Hide** method removes it. This is covered in detail in Chapter 13.

```vbnet
Private Sub btnOK_Click(ByVal sender As System.Object, _
    ByVal e As System.EventArgs) Handles btnOK.Click
        Dim frm2 As New frmSplash( )
        Dim Password As String
        Static Attempts As Short
' only allow 3 attempts before exiting
        If Attempts = 2 Then
                Me.Hide( )                      'hide the current form
                MessageBox.Show("Logon aborted", "Failed logon", _
                    MessageBoxButtons.OK, MessageBoxIcon.Error)
                Application.Exit( )
        Else
                Password = LCase(txtPassword.Text)  ' make lower case
                If Password <> "latinum" Then
' incorrect password
                MessageBox.Show("Password not recognised", "Password check", _
                    MessageBoxButtons.OK, MessageBoxIcon.Error)
                Else
' correct password so enter the system
                        MessageBox.Show("Welcome to Web Systems International", _
                            "Password Check", MessageBoxButtons.OK, _
                            MessageBoxIcon.Information)
                        Me.Hide( )
                        frm2 = New frmSplash( )
                        frm2.Show( )
                End If
                Attempts = Attempts + 1
        End If
End Sub

Private Sub btnCancel_Click(ByVal sender As System.Object, _
    ByVal e As System.EventArgs) Handles btnCancel.Click
' end the application
```

```
MessageBox.Show("Logon aborted", "Failed logon", _
    MessageBoxButtons.OK, MessageBoxIcon.Error)
    Application.Exit( )          ' end the application
End Sub
```

Note that the variable *Attempts* is **Static** and therefore will retain its value after the event procedure has completed, and is not re–initialized every time it is run. The password is not case sensitive, therefore the **LCase** function is used to convert the text typed into lower case. The password which we are looking for is *latinum*.

The application is exited by using the **Exit** method:

```
Application.Exit( )
```

The application functions well, but the event procedure for the *OK* button is rather too long and therefore difficult to debug, and it would be awkward to reuse the code elsewhere if there was a further logon process to use a restricted part of the system. We can break this application down into more manageable, reusable chunks by creating two new procedures.

Creating a procedure

The first procedure we are going to create is called *checkPassword*. The procedure template is shown below:

```
Private Sub checkPassword( )
......
End Sub
```

After you have typed the first line, the **End Sub** is automatically added. The second procedure we are going to create is called *exitApplication*.

These procedures can be called in two ways: you can either specify just the name of the procedure, or the name preceded by the word **Call**, for example:.

```
exitApplication( )
```

and

```
Call exitApplication( )
```

do exactly the same thing, but it is better to use the **Call** keyword to make it absolutely clear that you are calling a procedure.

The **Click** event handler for the *OK* button can now be rewritten:

```
Private Sub btnOK_Click(ByVal sender As System.Object, _
    ByVal e As System.EventArgs) Handles btnOK.Click
        Static Attempts As Short
' only allow 3 attempts before exiting
        If Attempts = 2 Then
            Call exitApplication( )
        Else : Call checkPassword( )
        End If
        Attempts = Attempts + 1
End Sub
```

The **Click** event procedure for the *Cancel* button can be rewritten:

```
Private Sub btnCancel_Click(ByVal sender As System.Object, _
    ByVal e As System.EventArgs) Handles btnCancel.Click
' end the application
        Call exitApplication( )
End Sub
```

Finally we have to write the code for our own procedures. The *ExitApplication* is called in the event handlers for the *OK* and also the *Cancel* button It displays a message box and closes the applications:

```
Private Sub exitApplication( )
    Me.Hide( )
    MessageBox.Show("Logon aborted", "Failed logon", _
        MessageBoxButtons.OK, MessageBoxIcon.Error)
    Application.Exit( ) ' end the application
End Sub
```

The *CheckPassword* procedure is shown below:

```
Private Sub checkPassword( )
    Dim Password As String
    Dim frm2 As New frmSplash( )
    Password = LCase(txtPassword.Text) ' make lower case
    If Password <> "latinum" Then
        ' incorrect password
        MessageBox.Show("Password not recognised", "Password check", _
            MessageBoxButtons.OK, MessageBoxIcon.Error)
    Else
    ' correct password so enter the system
        MessageBox.Show("Welcome to Web Systems International", _
            "Password Check", MessageBoxButtons.OK, _
            MessageBoxIcon.Information)
        Me.Hide( )
        frm2 = New frmSplash( )
        frm2.Show( )
    End If
End Sub
```

Functionally the application performs as before, but it has been broken down into more manageable pieces, which means that it can be debugged more easily and the procedures we have written can be reused within this application or another.

Passing parameters

Sometimes you may wish to pass information to a procedure, so that it can take different action depending on the data which is passed to it.

In the next application shown running in Figure 7.5, a mark between 0 and 100 is entered. The number of students and the average grade are calculated and displayed.

Three error conditions are handled in this application:

- A non-numeric input.
- A negative grade.
- A grade greater than 100.

Depending on which of these errors occurs a different dialog is displayed.

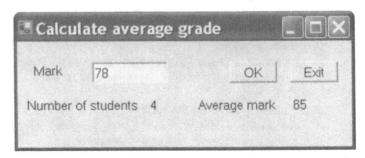

Figure 7.5 *Calculating average grades.*

Figure 7.6 shows the dialog when a grade over 100 is entered.

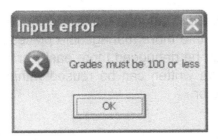

Figure 7.6 *The error dialog.*

When one of these errors is detected, a procedure is called and an integer is passed to it. Depending on the value of this integer a different error dialog is displayed. The advantage of using a procedure to handle the display of the error dialog is that you may want to display the same dialog from several different places in your application. If you want to make a change to the message you only have to do so in one place. If you do not perform your error handling centrally within a single procedure, it is easy make a mistake and to have slightly different text displayed when you want exactly the same message to be displayed. Users are quick to pick up on inconsistencies in applications, which gives a very unprofessional feel to the program.

To create this application:

- Change the name of the **Button** control to *btnOK*
- Change the name of the **TextBox** control to *txtMark*.
- Change the name of the two **Label** controls which display the number of students and the average mark to *lblNumberOfStudents* and *lblAverageMark*.

The procedure called *ErrorMessage* takes a single **Short** parameter and depending on its value displays a different error message. The procedure is shown below:

```
Private Sub ErrorMessage(ByVal shtErrorNumber As Short)
' Display a different error message depending on the value passed
    Dim message As String
    Select Case shtErrorNumber
        Case 1 : message = "Must enter an integer value"
        Case 2 : message = "Must input a positive integer"
        Case 3 : message = "Grades must be 100 or less"
        Case Else : message = "unknown input error"
    End Select
    MessageBox.Show(message, "Input error", _
        MessageBoxButtons.OK, MessageBoxIcon.Error)
End Sub
```

This procedure is called from three places in the application in the event handler for the *OK* button.

```
Private Sub btnOK_Click(ByVal sender As System.Object, _
    ByVal e As System.EventArgs) Handles btnOK.Click
    Static shtNumberOfStudents As Short
    Static shtTotal As Short
    Dim shtMark As Short
    Try
        shtMark = CShort(txtMark.Text)
        If shtMark < 0 Then
            Call ErrorMessage(2)
        ElseIf shtMark > 100 Then
            Call ErrorMessage(3)
            txtMark.Text = ""  ' clear the input TextBox
        Else
            shtTotal = shtTotal + shtMark
```

```
                shtNumberOfStudents = shtNumberOfStudents + 1
                lblNumberOfStudents.Text = CStr(shtNumberOfStudents)
                lblAverageMark.Text = CStr(shtTotal / shtNumberOfStudents)
            End If
    Catch ex As System.InvalidCastException
            Call ErrorMessage(1)            ' only come here if CShort fails
        End Try
        txtMark.Text = "" ' clear the input TextBox
        txtMark.Focus( )
End Sub
```

An attempt is made to convert the text in the **TextBox** into a **Short** value using the **CShort** function. Since this line is within a **Try..End Try** clause, if the conversion fails, an exception, a type of recoverable error, is produced which transfers control to the **Catch** clause which calls the *ErrorMessage* procedure with a parameter of 1. The **Catch** clause is not executed if an exception does not occur and the value input is successfully converted to a **Short** value.

If the conversion is successfully achieved a check is made to see if the value is less than 0. If it is, the *ErrorMessage* procedure is called with a parameter of 2.

A final check is made to see if the value is greater than 100. If it is the *ErrorMessage* procedure is called with a parameter of 3.

If the input is valid, the number of students is increased by 1 and the new average mark calculated and displayed.

The **TextBox** is cleared and the focus is returned to it for further input using the **Focus** method of that control.

Creating functions

A function is very similar to a procedure, the difference is that it returns a value. We have already seen some standard Visual Basic functions, for example the **Now** function returns the current date and time.

```
txtDateAndTime = Now
```

The **Now** function does not take any parameters, but both Visual Basic defined functions and your own functions can be passed parameters, for example:

```
Dim strString As String
Dim intCount As Integer
strString = "1234"
intCount = CInt(strString)
```

The **CInt** function is a standard Visual Basic function which takes the **String** *strString* as a parameter and returns an **Integer** value. The variable *intCount* is given the value returned by that function.

Since functions return a value they need to have a defined type; in the function shown below, the function *Biggest* takes three **Integer** parameters. After the declaration of the parameters, the function type is specified, in this case **Integer**.

```
Public Function Biggest(a As Integer, b As Integer, c As Integer) As Integer
    Biggest = a
    If b > Biggest Then Biggest = b
    If c > Biggest Then Biggest = c
End Function
```

The value returned is the value of the variable which has the function name, in this case *Biggest*.

This function can be called as follows:

```
Dim Result As Integer
Result = Biggest(2333, 87, 878)
```

The value returned is the largest number passed to the function, 2333.

Call by reference and call by value

There are two ways in which information can be passed to a procedure or a function, call by reference and call by value. The default used in Visual Basic is pass by value – if you do not add **ByVal** or **ByRef** Visual Basic automatically adds **ByVal** for you.

When a parameter is passed to a procedure by reference the address of that data is passed, so that if you make any changes to that data item in the called procedure it will be changed in the calling procedure. This has some interesting repercussions on the scope of variables, since if you define a variable in a procedure it can only be changed in that procedure, unless you pass it by reference to another procedure where it can also be changed.

If you pass a variable by value a copy of that variable is made and passed to the called procedure. If you make any changes to that variable in the called procedure the original variable in the calling procedure is not changed.

Let us see how this works in practice by using a small procedure which uses pass by reference.

```
Public Sub Power(ByRef intValue As Integer, ByVal intPow As Integer)
' raise intValue to the power intPow and return the result in intValue
    Dim c As Integer
    Dim intResult As Integer
    If intPow = 0 Then
        intValue = 1 ' anything to the power zero is one
' if intPow is 1 no action required
    ElseIf intPow > 1 Then
        intResult = intValue ' anything to the power one is itself
        For c = 1 To intPow – 1
            intResult = intResult * intValue
```

```
            Next c
            intValue = intResult
     End If
End Sub
```

This procedure is passed two **Integer** values called *intValue* and *intPow*. The value *intValue* is raised to the power *intPow* and the result returned in *intValue*; if for example *Value* is 3 and *Pow* is 2, the procedure calculates 3^2 or 9. This could be called by the statement:

```
Call Power(intA, intB)
```

where both *intA* and *intB* are **Integer** variables defined within the calling procedure which correspond with *intValue* and *intPow* in the called procedure *Power*. Changing *intValue* in *Power* results in the variable *intA* changing, even though *intA* is defined as a local variable to the calling procedure. If the procedure *Power* was altered so that both parameters were passed by value, and the result printed in the Output window at the end of *Power* as shown, just before the **End Sub** statement:

```
System.Console.WriteLine(CStr(intValue)) ' correct value is displayed
```

the correct result would be displayed in the Output window from *Power*. However, if you printed the variable *intA* immediately after the call to *Power* in the calling procedure:

```
Call Power(intA, intB)
System.Console.WriteLine(CStr(intA))      ' value is unchanged
```

the variable *intA* would be unchanged, since only a copy of it had been passed to *Power*. If the Output window is not visible select the **View | Other Windows | Output** menu option.

Note that to pass a variable by value (and to override the default of pass by reference), the parameter must be preceded by the **ByVal** keyword.

Where possible, call by reference should be avoided, since it alters the scope of variables and if you find that a variable has an unexpected value when debugging, it makes it harder to find out where the problem occurred. It is often possible to design a procedure in a different way so that call by reference is not used. The *Power* procedure could easily be changed to become an **Integer** function which returns the result and has two parameters passed to it by value. The only situation where it is not possible to use this approach is when you want to return more than one value from a procedure. In these circumstances perhaps it is better to write two functions rather than one procedure and to use pass by value.

Using a start–up procedure

All of the applications we have seen so far have used a form as the start–up object. You can choose which form starts the application or specify a start–up procedure which must be called **Main**. To specify the start–up object select a project in the Solution Explorer and then choose the **View | Property Pages** menu option to display the dialog shown in Figure 7.7.

The advantage of using a **Main** procedure to start an application is that the opening form of an application often contains a lot of controls and may take some time to load. If you use a **Main** procedure you can display a splash screen welcoming the user and load the other forms into memory, so that when the user closes the opening splash screen, the forms appear quickly. It does not actually make the application run any faster, it just avoids a wait at the start of the application while the initial form is loaded.

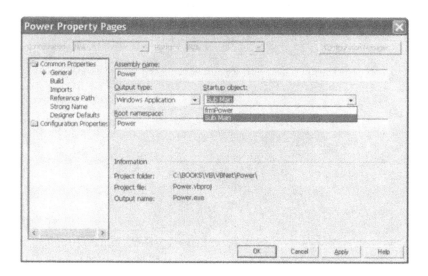

Figure 7.7 *Specifying the start–up object.*

The **Main** procedure is normally placed in a separate module. These modules are used to hold Visual Basic procedures and functions which are not related directly to the events which occur on a form. To create a new module select the **Project | Add Component** and choose the **Module** icon from the Add New Item dialog displayed. The outline for the **Main** procedure is:

```
Public Sub Main( )
' add statements here
End Sub
```

Chapter 8

Classes and Objects

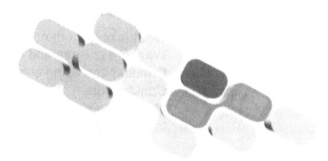

Introduction

One of the most important aspects of Visual Basic .NET is the introduction of language constructs which allow you to write object oriented programs. When I first read that this version of Visual Basic was to be object oriented I was initially sceptical, but my fears were not justified. Visual Basic is now capable of creating fully object oriented application in a similar way to the more traditional object oriented languages such as C++ and Java. Object orientation is often presented as a complex, difficult subject, but the ideas behind it are fairly straightforward to understand, it is the application of these ideas which is difficult. Problems often arise if you have a strong background in programming using alternative techniques such as structured programming. This chapter does not cover every aspect of object oriented programming which is available in Visual Basic but it does introduce the main concepts and show how they are applied. In this chapter we are going to look at:

- What is object orientation?
- What are classes and objects?
- Creating and using classes and objects.
- Constructors.
- Method overloading.
- Inheritance.

What is object orientation?

The ideas behind object orientation are ones that most people are already familiar with. Increasingly most of the domestic machinery and the cars we use are made up of a collection of parts, for example a bicycle is made up of a frame, wheels, seat, handlebars and so on. If one of these pieces is damaged we tend to just replace it rather than trying to repair it. We know that if we buy a wheel of the right dimensions and fit it into the frame it will work. We do not have to buy the spokes, the rim and the hub and build it. Similarly, if you want to build a PC, you can do so from a relatively small number of parts such as a main board, a processor, a disk drive, a CD drive, memory, a graphics card, and a case. You do not need to buy a selection of chips and a soldering iron. If the graphics card fails, we just buy another one and replace the defective part. Increasingly cars are being built like this, since it is cheaper and easier to replace a defective or damaged part rather than pay an expensive mechanic to fix it (if we ignore the environmental costs). In addition, using a single replacement part is likely to be more reliable than building one from components.

This sort of approach has gained wide acceptance and has many advantages. It is usually much quicker and easier to build from a set of standard parts rather than producing parts from the most basic elements. The cost of employing people is usually high so there is a cost saving if the time needed to build an item is reduced and there is the additional benefit that reliable items can be built faster. You do not need to understand how a disk drive works to be able to upgrade the drive on your PC. There are some disadvantages to this approach, the level of skill required to build the basic components is high and for them to be reliable they must be meticulously tested so they can be used with a high degree of confidence. If you are intent on using an existing component it may not do exactly what you want, so you could end up compromising your design because of the need to use existing controls.

One of the most important aspects is that these basic units can be put together in different combinations to build different machines, for example many cars share the same basic control, such as engine and suspension, but are sold as different vehicles because they have a different body shell. One of the key ideas behind object orientation is the idea that existing classes can be combined to produce a variety of complex products.

These ideas have been accepted in the engineering world for decades and although object orientation has been discussed since the 1970s it has only recently begun to be widely adopted. A key concept of object orientation is that software applications can be based on a combination of existing classes rather than writing every application individually. There are dozens of different word processors in use today; each of them took hundreds of man-years to write and each of them does roughly the same thing. For example, each of them has a facility for searching for a particular piece of text, this has been re-written for every word processor. It would be much simpler if the software engineers creating the word processors could use an existing class which had the capabilities of doing this. The software designers would not need to know how this class worked, just that it produced the correct result.

Many companies already have libraries of procedures which are available to their in-house software engineers. These are usually in a format which does not make it possible for them to be easily used by third parties. For the same reasons it is difficult for companies to buy a library of procedures since its format and scope may not conform to that used in the company. An object oriented approach defines classes in a standard way which allows re-use to be achieved far more easily as we will see next.

What are classes and objects?

A class is the description of an object and how it behaves, for example, if you were designing an application for a library, one of the classes you are likely to create could be called *clsBook*. The *clsBook* class would have a set of properties or attributes which describe a book, for example, the author of the book, the title of the book, the cost, its location in the library and whether it is on loan or not. In addition there would be a set of operations or methods which can be carried out on the books in this class, for example, a method to display all details of the book, and another to indicate if it was on loan or not.

The *clsBook* class describes what characteristics a book has and what can be done to it. A *clsBook* object refers to a particular book rather than just a description of it. A *clsBook* object is sometimes called an instance of a class, for example this book is a *clsBook* object or an instance of the *clsBook* class.

All of the objects of a class share the same properties but there will be different values for these properties. The title property for this book is *Essential VB .NET fast*. Similarly every book object has the same set of methods that operate on the properties, for example, the method which displays book details will show different output for every object.

In the next section we are going to see how to create the *clsBook* class and how to create instances, that is objects of that class.

Creating and using classes and objects

The next application we are going to look at creates a class called *clsBook* and shows some *clsBook* objects in action. At first it can seem difficult to create and use objects and so to simplify this the application does not have a visual user interface. It is a Console Application; it simply displays its output in the Console window.

To create the application:

- Select the **File | New | Project** menu option and clock on the **Empty Project** icon. Name the project *Book*.
- Select the **Project | Add Class** menu option and name the class *clsBook*. An outline class is created as shown below:

```
Public Class clsBook

End Class
```

To test the class we will need to create some objects of the *clsBook* class, to do this we need to create a module.

- Select the **Project | Add Component** menu option and click on the **Module** option. Name the module **Main**.
- Add a new procedure to the **Main** module. An outline procedure is created as shown below:

```
Module Main
    Sub Main( )

    End Sub
End Module
```

The **Main** method is the place where the application will start running.

This has created the framework for the application, the next stage is to define the class

The clsBook class

When defining a class there are two aspects to consider: what attributes are required; and what operations are required, that is what methods are needed.

The attributes

Most of the attributes required are fairly intuitive. They define the characteristics of a book:

- The title of the book.
- The author of the book.
- The location of the book in the library.
- The name of the borrower.
- The return date of the book if it has been borrowed.
- The loan type of the book, either, reference only (not available for loan), seven-day loan or normal loan which is 28 days.

The first four items are **String** type, the return date is of type **Date**. The loan type could be stored as a **String**, but to save space it is saved as a variable of type **Short**. To make it easier to work with four constants have been defined. It is easier to refer to a loan type called *reference* rather than 0. The definitions of the constants and instance variables are shown below:

```
Public Class clsBook
    Dim strTitle As String
    Dim strAuthor As String
    Dim strLocation As String
```

```
Dim strBorrower As String
Dim datReturnDate As Date
Dim shtLoanType As Short
Const reference As Short = 0
Const sevenDayLoan As Short = 1
Const normalLoan As Short = 2
Const unknown As Short = 3
```

This completes the definition of the attributes or instance variables. Every *clsBook* object has its own set of attributes assigned to appropriate values for that object, for example, every object will have a title attribute which contains a different **String**.

Referencing the attributes

When you create an object of type *clsBook* you need to be able to reference the attributes of that object. You could do this simply by making the attributes **Public** – they would then be visible anywhere in the application, however a better way is to use the **Property** statement. This statement for accessing the *strTitle* attribute is shown below:

```
Public Property title( ) As String
    Get
            Return (strTitle)
    End Get
    Set(ByVal Value As String)
            strTitle = Value
    End Set
End Property
```

This statement consists of two parts, the **Get** and the **Set** clause. The **Get** clause returns the current value of the attribute *strTitle*. The **Set** clause assigns it a value which is passed to it. The property is called *title* which means that when you create a *clsBook* object you can refer to the *title* property. This property will appear as an available property in the available IntelliSense options.

Similar **Property** statements are needed for the *strAuthor* and *strLocation* attributes. These are shown below:

```
Public Property author( ) As String
        Get
                Return (strAuthor)
        End Get
        Set(ByVal Value As String)
                strAuthor = Value
        End Set
End Property

Public Property location( ) As String
        Get
                Return (strLocation)
        End Get
        Set(ByVal Value As String)
                strLocation = Value
        End Set
End Property
```

ReadOnly and WriteOnly properties

The *strBorrower* property is a little different. A borrower is assigned to a book only when it is borrowed, at the same time the return date is calculated. Therefore this property is read only: it cannot be changed. To reflect this the **ReadOnly** reserved word is added to the **Property** statement and the **Set** clause is omitted as shown below:

```
Public ReadOnly Property borrower( ) As String
        Get
                Return (strBorrower)
        End Get
End Property
```

Similarly the *datReturnDate* property is return only as this is calculated when a book is borrowed. It is dependent on the date it is borrowed and the type of book, some books are on seven-day loan while others are available for 28-day loan. The **Property** statement for this attribute is shown below:

```
Public ReadOnly Property returnDate( ) As Date
     Get
          Return (datReturnDate)
     End Get
End Property
```

If a property may only be written and not read, the **WriteOnly** reserved word is used instead of **ReadOnly** and the **Get** clause is omitted.

The shtLoanType attribute

The **Properties** statement for the attributes we have looked at have done nothing except set or return the attributes, however you can add any code you wish to this statement. The *LoanType* property is stored as a **Short** data type to save space, however for convenience it can be referred to by a **String**. This **String** may be either *Reference*, *7 day loan* or *normal loan*. In the **Get** clause the **Short** attribute is converted to the corresponding **String** which is returned. The process is carried out in reverse in the **Set** clause. The properties statement for this attribute is shown below:

```
Public Property LoanType( ) As String
     Get
          If shtLoanType = reference Then
               Return "Reference"
          ElseIf shtLoanType = sevenDayLoan Then
               Return "7 day loan"
          ElseIf shtLoanType = normalLoan Then
               Return "normal loan"
          Else
               Return "Unknown type"
          End If
     End Get
     Set(ByVal Value As String)
```

```
            If Value = "Reference" Then
                    shtLoanType = reference
            Elself Value = "7 Day Loan" Then
                    shtLoanType = sevenDayLoan
            Elself Value = "normal loan" Then
                    shtLoanType = normalLoan
            Else
                    shtLoanType = unknown
            End If
        End Set
End Property
```

The methods we have written so far have been concerned with accessing the attributes, but additional methods are needed to make this into a working application. We are going to look at three methods.

The onLoan method

The *OnLoan* method returns a **Boolean**, this is **True** if the item is currently on loan and **False** if it is not. If the book is for reference it cannot be on loan. Also, if it is available for loan, and there is no borrower it is not on loan.

The code for this method is shown below:

```
Public Function onLoan( ) As Boolean
    If strBorrower = Nothing Or shtLoanType = reference Then
            Return False
    Else
            Return True
    End If
End Function
```

The borrow method

This method is passed the name of the borrower as a **String**. It checks to see if the book is reference only and not available for loan, or if it is already on loan to another reader. If it is available for loan, the name passed to the method is assigned to the *strBorrower* attribute and the return date is calculated as either 7 or 28 days from the current date (given by the **Now** function) depending on whether the loan type is seven day loan or normal loan. The method is shown below:

```
Public Sub borrow(ByVal name As String)
    If shtLoanType <> reference And strBorrower = Nothing Then
        strBorrower = name
        If shtLoanType = sevenDayLoan Then
            datReturnDate = Now.AddDays(7)
        Else
            datReturnDate = Now.AddDays(28)
        End If
    End If
End Sub
```

The displayDetails method

The final method returns details of the object as a **String**. The method is shown below:

```
Public Function displayDetails( ) As String
    Dim strMsg As String
    strMsg = "The author is " & strAuthor & vbCrLf
    strMsg = strMsg & "The title is " & strTitle & vbCrLf
    strMsg = strMsg & "The location is " & strLocation & vbCrLf
    strMsg = strMsg & "loan type is " & LoanType( ) & vbCrLf
    If onLoan( ) = True Then
        strMsg = strMsg & "On loan" & " to " & strBorrower
        strMsg = strMsg & " return date is " & datReturnDate
    Else
        strMsg = strMsg & "not on loan"
    End If
    strMsg = strMsg & vbCrLf
    Return strMsg
End Function
```

Note the use of the *onLoan* method to determine the loan status of the book and to add an appropriate

method. If a book is on loan the name of the borrower and the return date are added to the **String** which is returned.

Creating objects

So far we have created the *clsBook* class which is a definition of what attributes are needed to fully describe a book in a library and what operations are likely to be performed on it.   One of the criticisms of object oriented design is that a lot of work is needed before quite simple operations can be carried out. There is some truth in this criticism and the real benefits really only become apparent for larger applications, or applications where existing class libraries can be used.

Now that the *clsBook* class has been defined we can create some objects of this type. We do this in the **Main** method. Creating objects is a two stage process. The first stage defines an object as being of the specified class, for example:

```
Dim objUseful As clsBook
```

The second stage instantiates the object, that is allocates memory for it, initializes attributes and runs a special method called a constructor, for example:

```
objUseful = New clsBook( )
```

creates the *objUseful* object or instance of the *clsBook* class. The attributes and methods of this object are used by giving the name of the object a period and then the name of the attribute or method. Methods should have opening and closing round brackets after them even if no parameters are being passed. The code below allocates some values to the attributes of the object and the *borrow* method specifies the name of the lender and also sets up the return date by reference to today's date and the loan type:

```
objUseful.title = "Useful Toil"
objUseful.author = "John Burnett"
objUseful.location = "SOC45987"
objUseful.LoanType = "normal loan"
objUseful.borrow("L.Blomfeld")
```

We can check that the object has been setup correctly by using the *displayDetails* method and displaying the **String** it returns using the **System.Console.WriteLine** method which displays its output in the Console window:

```
System.Console.WriteLine(objUseful.displayDetails)
```

The output is shown in Figure 8.1.

```
■ C:\BOOKS\VB\VBNet\Chapter8\OO\bin\OO.exe          _ □ ×
The author is John Burnett
The title is Useful Toil
The location is SOC45987
loan type is Normal loan
On loan to L.Blomfeld   return date is 28/03/2002 10:12:54
```

Figure 8.1 *Displaying a single object's details.*

You are not limited to creating a single object you can create as many objects of type *clsBook* as you wish, for example another object may be created as shown below:

```
Dim objWhen As clsBook
objWhen = New clsBook( )
objWhen.title = "When we were orphans"
objWhen.author = "Kazuo Ishiguro"
objWhen.location = "LIT77493"
objWhen.LoanType = "7 Day Loan"
objWhen.borrow("Alan Paton")
System.Console.WriteLine(objWhen.displayDetails)
```

The output by running this application is shown in Figure 8.2.

```
■ C:\BOOKS\VB\VBNet\Chapter8\OO\bin\OO.exe         _ □ ×
The author is John Burnett
The title is Useful Toil
The location is SOC45987
loan type is Normal loan
On loan to L.Blomfeld  return date is 28/03/2002 10:12:54

The author is Kazuo Ishiguro
The title is When we were orphans
The location is LIT77493
loan type is 7 day loan
On loan to Alan Paton  return date is 07/03/2002 10:12:54
```

Figure 8.2 *Displaying details of two objects.*

Constructors

When an object is instantiated a special method called a constructor is executed. In the example we have looked at so far we have not explicitly written a constructor method we have relied on Visual Basic to initialize our attributes for us. It is often helpful to create a constructor which does some basic initialisation of attributes the moment the object is created, for example the majority of books in the library are going to be for normal 28-day loan, therefore it would be helpful if we could by default assign the loan type to this. The constructor method is always called **New** and must be defined within the class it applies to. The constructor for the *clsBook* class is shown below:

```
Public Sub New( )
    shtLoanType = normalLoan
End Sub
```

This method is always executed when an object is created.

Method overloading

One of the useful features of object orientation is method overloading. You may have more than one method with the same name. Your application is able to decide which one you want to use on the basis of the parameter list you supply. You can overload constructor methods, for example, if you wanted to supply the full details of a *clsBook* object when you instantiated the object you need a constructor method which is passed this information:

```
Public Sub New(ByVal title As String, ByVal author As String, _
    ByVal location As String, ByVal loan As String)
        strTitle = title
        strAuthor = author
        strLocation = location
        If loan = "Reference" Then
                shtLoanType = reference
        ElseIf loan = "7 Day Loan" Then
                shtLoanType = sevenDayLoan
        ElseIf loan = "normal loan" Then
                shtLoanType = normalLoan
        Else
                shtLoanType = unknown
        End If
End Sub
```

This method is supplied with the title, author, location and loan type and sets up the corresponding attributes. You would use the constructor as shown below:

```
Dim objWhen As clsBook
objWhen = New clsBook("When we were orphans", _
    "Kazuo Ishiguro", "LIT4932", "normal loan")
```

If you wished to produce a further overloaded constructor method which only required the author and title to be passed as parameters:

```
Public Sub New(ByVal title As String, ByVal author As String)
        strTitle = title
```

```
    strAuthor = author
End Sub
```

This constructor could be called by the following statements:

```
Dim objBlack As clsBook
objBlack = New clsBook("Black and Blue", "Ian Rankin")
```

Any method can be overloaded not only constructors.

Inheritance

One of the key aspects of object orientation system design is inheritance. If a class inherits from another class it has all its attributes and methods and in addition you can add further attributes and methods. The need to do this is surprisingly common, consider for example our *clsBook* class. If the library also wanted to loan video tapes it would need all of the same information and methods, but in addition an attribute which gave the running time and another which gave the format of the tape. If we can inherit all of the methods and attributes from the *clsBook* class there is very little work to do to extend our system to handle videos. To inherit from a class add the reserved word **Inherits** followed by the name of the class to inherit from as shown below:

```
Public Class clsVideo
  Inherits clsBook
    Dim strVideoFormat As String
    Dim shtTime As Short

    Public Property time( ) As Short
        Get
            Return (shtTime)
        End Get
        Set(ByVal Value As Short)
            shtTime = Value
        End Set
    End Property
```

```
Public Property format( ) As String
        Get
                Return (format)
        End Get
        Set(ByVal Value As String)
                strVideoFormat = Value
        End Set
    End Property
End Class
```

The new class *clsVideo* has all the functionality of the superclass *clsBook* and in addition two new attributes which give the time and format of the video. Note that you cannot selectively inherit attributes and methods: everything is inherited.

In the **Main** method you can create an instance of the new class *clsVideo* and use the methods defined in the superclass clsBook:

```
Dim objMatrix As clsVideo
objMatrix = New clsVideo( )
objMatrix.title = "The Matrix"
objMatrix.author = "Warner Bros"
objMatrix.location = "VID25558"
objMatrix.LoanType = "7 Day Loan"
objMatrix.time = 130
objMatrix.format = "VHS"
```

Object orientation is a large area and this chapter has not covered all the aspects of it which are available in Visual Basic .NET, but it does cover the essential features which will allow you to start creating object oriented applications.

Chapter 9

Further Windows Controls

Introduction

We have already seen many controls for creating Windows applications in action. In this chapter we are going to look at some more of the standard Windows controls and how to use them, in particular:

- The **Timer** control.
- The **ListBox** control.
- The **ComboBox** control.
- The **MonthCalendar** control.
- The **DateTimePicker** control.
- The **TrackBar** control.
- The **RichTextBox** control.

The Timer control

The **Timer** control allows you to trigger an event at regular intervals. In the application we are going to look at, a **Timer** control is used for updating a clock. It does not matter where you place the control since it is not visible at run–time.

- To display the clock a **Label** control is used to display the time. The name of the control is changed to *lblTime*.
- Add a **Timer** control to the application, change its name to **timTimer** and set the **Enabled** property to **True**.
- Set the **Interval** property of the **Timer** to the length of the time between the **Tick** events in milliseconds, 1000 in this case so the clock display is updated every second.

The code for the **Timer** control **Tick** event is shown below.

```
Private Sub timTimer_Tick(ByVal sender As System.Object, _
    ByVal e As System.EventArgs) Handles timTimer.Tick
        lblTime.Text = Now
End Sub
```

This event handler is run every second and displays the current date and time.

The ListBox control

The **ListBox** control has a very similar behaviour to the **ComboBox** control, but a different appearance.

To see how this control is used we are going to develop the application shown running in Figure 9.1. The **ListBox** control displays a list of sports which are added to the list at run–time. You can select one or more of the sports: as you do so, the sports you have selected are displayed in the **TextBox** control at the bottom of the form. You can add a new sport to the list by typing it into the **TextBox** on the right of the form and clicking the *Add a new sport* button. You can delete one or more selected sports by clicking on the *Delete selected sports* button.

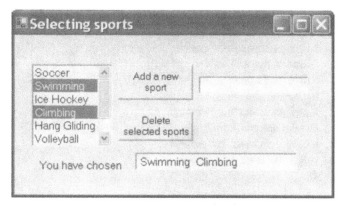

Figure 9.1 Using the **ListBox** control.

To create this application:

- Create a user interface similar to Figure 9.1.
- Change the name of the **ListBox** to *lstSports*.
- Change the name of the two buttons to *btnAdd* and *btnDelete*.
- Change the name of the **TextBox** where the new sports are typed to *txtNewSport*.
- Change the name of the **TextBox** which displays the chosen sports to *txtChosen.*
- To ensure that more than one item can be selected from the **ListBox** change the **SelectionMode** property from **Single** to **MultiExtended**. This property may also be set to **MultiSimple**, which allows multiple selection of all entries between a selected item and another item which is selected with the Shift key pressed.
- Set the **Text** properties of the two **TextBox** controls to "", so that no text is displayed when the application starts.
- You can add items to a **ListBox** at design–time using the **Items** property, but in this application we are adding the items at run–time using the **Add** method in the Form Load event handler:

```
Private Sub Form1_Load(ByVal sender As System.Object, _
   ByVal e As System.EventArgs) Handles MyBase.Load
      lstSports.Items.Add("Soccer")
      lstSports.Items.Add("Swimming")
      lstSports.Items.Add("Ice Hockey")
      lstSports.Items.Add("Climbing")
      lstSports.Items.Add("Hiking")
      lstSports.Items.Add("Hang Gliding")
      lstSports.Items.Add("Volleyball")
      lstSports.Items.Add("Sleeping")
End Sub
```

The entries can be accessed at any time, for example the first item can be accessed by reference to *lstSports.Items(0).*

To add the sport typed into the *txtNewSport* **TextBox** to the **ListBox** when the *btnAdd* button is pressed:

```
Private Sub btnAdd_Click(ByVal sender As System.Object, _
    ByVal e As System.EventArgs) Handles btnAdd.Click
        lstSports.Items.Add(txtNewSport.Text)
        txtNewSport.Text = ""
End Sub
```

The text in the **TextBox** is also erased.

The number of selected items in a **ListBox** is given by the **Count** property. Each selected entry in the **ListBox** is stored in the **SelectedItems** property. The first item is stored in **SelectedItems**(0). For example the first selected item can be copied to a **String**:

```
Dim str as String
str = lstSports.SelectedItems(c)
```

When the *Sports* button is clicked, every selected item is added to the selected sports displayed in the *txtChosen* **TextBox** at the bottom of the form.

```
Private Sub lstSports_SelectedIndexChanged(ByVal sender _
    As System.Object, ByVal e As System.EventArgs) _
    Handles lstSports.SelectedIndexChanged
        Dim c As Short
        txtChosen.Text = ""
        For c = 0 To lstSports.SelectedItems.Count - 1
            txtChosen.Text = txtChosen.Text & " " & lstSports.SelectedItems(c) & " "
        Next c
End Sub
```

Finally, to activate the *btnDelete* button, the **Remove** method is used, this requires each of the selected items to be passed to it.

```
Private Sub btnDelete_Click(ByVal sender As System.Object, _
    ByVal e As System.EventArgs) Handles btnDelete.Click
        Dim c As Short
        For c = lstSports.SelectedItems.Count - 1 To 0 Step -1
            lstSports.Items.Remove(lstSports.SelectedItems(c))
        Next c
        txtChosen.Text = ""
End Sub
```

The ComboBox control

The **ComboBox** control has three distinct forms determined by the **DropDownStyle** property. This property can have three possible values:

- **Simple.** This version comprises a **TextBox** and a list which is always displayed. You can select an item or type your own text.
- **Dropdown**. This version has a **TextBox** and a list which drops down below it. You can select an item from the list or type your own text in the text box.
- **DropDownList.** This is the same as a **DropDown ComboBox** except that while you can select an item from the list you cannot type your own text.

The three different styles are shown in Figure 9.2.

Figure 9.2 *Simple, DropDown and DropDownList styles.*

The form which we want to use in this application is the **DropDownList ComboBox**, since this allows you to select an item, but not to type your own text.

The ComboBox application

The application we are going to develop next is shown in Figure 9.3 and uses the **ComboBox** and **PictureBox** controls. You can select one of the sports shown in the **ComboBox**; the corresponding picture is displayed in a **PictureBox** control and a **Label** control displays the name of the sport selected.

Figure 9.3 *The running application.*

The first stage in creating this application is to add the **PictureBox**, **ComboBox** and **Label** controls to the design form, so they are roughly in the positions shown in Figure 9.3.

The next stage is to set up some properties at design–time.

- The **Name** property of the **PictureBox** control is changed to *picSport*. The **ComboBox** name is changed to *cboSports* and the **Label** is changed to *lblSport*.
- The **ComboBox DropDownStyle** property is changed to **DropdownList**.
- The **Text** property of the form is changed to *Showing sports pictures*.
- The **SizeMode** property of the **PictureBox** control is changed to **StretchImage**, so that the picture resizes itself to fit the control.

You can add the options which are displayed in the **ComboBox** at design–time by using the **Items** property, but we are going to do this at run–time using some Visual Basic statements.

Handling events

The best place to add items to the ComboBox control is when the Form **Load** event occurs, the event handler for this is shown below:

```
Dim strFiles(4) As String
Private Sub Form1_Load(ByVal sender As System.Object, _
   ByVal e As System.EventArgs) Handles MyBase.Load
     Dim c As Short
     strFiles(0) = "Soccer"
     strFiles(1) = "Water skiing"
     strFiles(2) = "Swimming"
     strFiles(3) = "Climbing"
     strFiles(4) = "Hang gliding"
     For c = 0 To 4
          CboSports.Items.Add(strFiles(c))
     Next c
     CboSports.SelectedIndex = 1
End Sub
```

An array of strings is defined called *strFiles*. Each element contains the name of a sport. The name of the file containing the picture of that sport is stored in a file of the same name, for example the climbing picture is stored in *climbing.bmp*.

The names of the sports are added to the **ComboBox** control with the **Add** method.

The **SelectedIndex** property which indicates the selected item is assigned to 1. This statement causes a **SelectedIndexChanged** event to occur and the handler for this event is called. It is shown below:

```
Private Sub CboSports_SelectedIndexChanged(ByVal sender _
   As System.Object, ByVal e As System.EventArgs) _
```

```
Handles CboSports.SelectedIndexChanged
    PicSport.Image = System.Drawing.Image.FromFile("C:\Sports\" & _
    strFiles(CboSports.SelectedIndex) & ".bmp")
        lblSports.Text = CboSports.SelectedItem
End Sub
```

The name and location of the image to be displayed is made up of three elements: the folder containing the files; the name of the file, which is derived from the *strFiles* array element corresponding to the selected item; and a file extension, which is .bmp in this case. If you try this application for yourself you will need to ensure that you have some suitable pictures at the location you specify.

The **Text** property of the **Label** is assigned the text corresponding to the selected item (this could have been derived from the *strFiles* array, since these array elements are the same as the items listed in the **ComboBox** control.

The MonthCalendar control

Many applications need to display a calendar and to allow a date or a range of dates to be selected. The **MonthCalendar** control is a useful control which displays, in its simplest form, a month at a time.

The control in action is shown in Figure 9.4.

Figure 9.4 The *MonthCalendar* control.

There are a wide range of options available to change its appearance, for example:

- The **ShowToday** property displays today's date at the bottom of the calendar if set to **True**.
- Today's date is circled if the **ShowTodayCircle** property is **True**.
- The start day of the week can be changed from its default of Sunday by using the **FirstDayOfWeek** property.
- The **CalendarDimensions** property can be changed from its default of 1,1 to show more than one month in a grid pattern.

The key feature of this control is that a range of dates can be selected unlike the similar **DateTimePicker** control which only allows one date to be chosen. The two properties which can be used to read or set selected dates are **SelectionStart** and **SelectionEnd**. These two properties are shown in action below:

```
lblStartDate.Text = CStr(MonthCalendar1.SelectionStart)
lblFinishDate.Text = CStr(MonthCalendar1.SelectionEnd)
```

The dates are converted to strings and displayed in two **Label** controls. The maximum number of days which can be selected at any one time are determined by the **MaxSelectionCount** property. The earliest and latest date which may be selected are determined by the **MinDate** and **MaxDate** properties.

The DateTimePicker control

The **DateTimePicker** control is very flexible and allows you to display dates and times in a wide variety of formats, you can even add your own formats if you wish. Figure 9.5 shows **DateTimePicker** controls with the **Format** property set to **Long**, **Short** and **Time**.

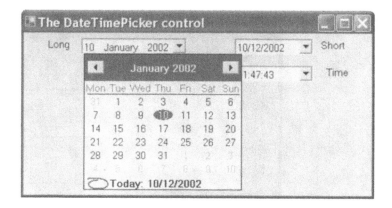

Figure 9.5 *Using the **DateTimePicker** control.*

Clicking on the down arrow alongside each control displays a dialog similar to the **MonthCalendar** control.

The date selected is returned in the **Value** property. If you wish you can also find out more specific detail such as the day of the week, the month, the year or even if the year is a leap year, for example:

```
lblDay.Text = CStr(DateTimePicker1.Value.Day)
```

This line of code assigns the day of the selected date to the **Text** property of the **Label** for display.

The TrackBar

The **TrackBar** control, is used to change a value by moving the position of the slider bar along a track. This is often used to create a user interface which is easier to use than requesting numbers to be entered.

In the example we are going to look at, the value of the red, green and blue components of the colour of the **TextBox** control are controlled by moving three sliders as shown in Figure 9.6. The current value of each slider is shown by the **Label** control on the right of each of the **TrackBar** controls.

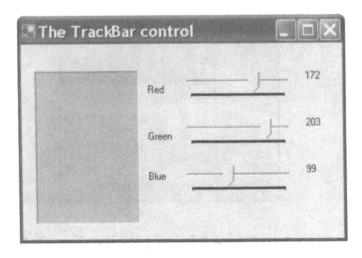

Figure 9.6 *Using the TrackBar to specify colours.*

To create this application:

- Create a user interface similar to that shown in Figure 9.6.
- Change the name of the **TrackBar** and **Label** controls to *tkbRed*, *tkbGreen*, *tkbBlue*, *lblRed*, *lblGreen* and *lblBlue*. Change the name of the **Text** control to *txtColour*.
- Set the **Minimum** and **Maximum** properties of the **TrackBar** controls to 0 and 255.

When a **TrackBar** moves the **Scroll** event occurs. The event procedures for the three sliders are shown below:

```
Private Sub tkbRed_Scroll(ByVal sender As System.Object, _
    ByVal e As System.EventArgs) Handles tkbRed.Scroll
        txtColour.BackColor = Color.FromArgb(255, tkbRed.Value, _
            tkbGreen.Value, tkbBlue.Value)
        lblRed.Text = CStr(tkbRed.Value)
End Sub

Private Sub tkbGreen_Scroll(ByVal sender As System.Object, _
    ByVal e As System.EventArgs) Handles tkbGreen.Scroll
        txtColour.BackColor = Color.FromArgb(255, tkbRed.Value, _
            tkbGreen.Value, tkbBlue.Value)
```

```
        lblGreen.Text = CStr(tkbGreen.Value)
End Sub

Private Sub tkbBlue_Scroll(ByVal sender As System.Object, _
    ByVal e As System.EventArgs) Handles tkbBlue.Scroll
        txtColour.BackColor = Color.FromArgb(255, tkbRed.Value, _
            tkbGreen.Value, tkbBlue.Value)
        lblBlue.Text = CStr(tkbBlue.Value)
End Sub
```

The **FromArgb** method of the **Color** class returns a **Color** object which is assigned to the **BackColor** property of the **TextBox**. This method takes four parameters, the opacity and the red, green and blue components of the colour. All these values are between 0 and 255. An opacity of 255 indicates a completely opaque colour.

To make the application start in a professional manner some initial values must be assigned to the controls, this is done in the **Load** event for the form:

```
Private Sub Form1_Load(ByVal sender As System.Object, _
    ByVal e As System.EventArgs) Handles MyBase.Load
        tkbRed.Value = 0
        tkbGreen.Value = 0
        tkbBlue.Value = 0
        txtColour.BackColor = Color.FromArgb(255, tkbRed.Value, _
        tkbGreen.Value, tkbBlue.Value)
        lblRed.Text = CStr(tkbRed.Value)
        lblGreen.Text = CStr(tkbGreen.Value)
        lblBlue.Text = CStr(tkbBlue.Value)
End Sub
```

This ensures that the **TrackBar** positions, and the text in the **Label** and **TextBox** controls are consistent when the application starts.

Most aspects of the control can be configured such as the **SmallChange** and **LargeChange** values, which determine how far the slider moves when it is dragged or the mouse clicked on one side of it. The **TrackBar** can be vertical rather than the default of horizontal if its **Orientation** property is changed.

The RichTextBox control

The **RichTextBox** control is an extended version of the **TextBox** control: unlike the **TextBox** it can display text in a variety of fonts and sizes in the same control.

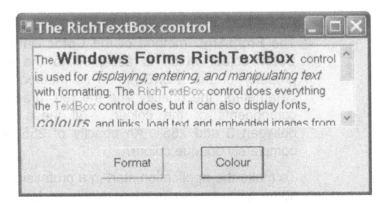

Figure 9.7 *Using the RichTextBox control.*

In a **TextBox** the **Font** property applies to all the text which it displays. The **RichTextBox** control has a number of properties which control text formatting, but these only apply to selected text.

The application which we are going to develop to see this control in action is shown in Figure 9.7.
Clicking on the *Format* button opens a **FontDialog** for font selection. Clicking on the *Colour* button opens a **ColorDialog** control for colour selection.
To create the application:

- Create a user interface similar to that shown in Figure 9.7. In addition add a **FontDialog** and **ColorDialog** control. These are not visible at run time.
- Change the names of the dialogs to *dlgFont* and *dlgColor*.

- Change the names of the buttons to *btnFormat* and *btnColour* and the **RichTextBox** to *rxtText*.
- Write the code for the click procedures for the two buttons as shown below:

```
Private Sub btnFormat_Click(ByVal sender As System.Object, _
    ByVal e As System.EventArgs) Handles btnFormat.Click
        dlgFont.ShowDialog( )          ' display the FontDialog
        rxtText.SelectionFont = dlgFont.Font
End Sub

Private Sub btnColour_Click(ByVal sender As System.Object, _
    ByVal e As System.EventArgs) Handles btnColour.Click
        dlgColor.ShowDialog( )         ' display the ColorDialog
        rxtText.SelectionColor = dlgColor.Color
End Sub
```

To change the font of the selected text the **SelectionFont** property is assigned to the **Font** chosen from the **FontDialog**. Similarly the colour of the selected text can be changed using the colour chosen from the **ColorDialog** and the **SelectionColor** property of the **RichTextBox**.

The **RichTextBox** is a powerful versatile control which can be used for all text manipulation. It is straightforward to write the supporting code for operations such as searching for characters as well as formatting the font and colour of text.

Chapter 10

Web Applications

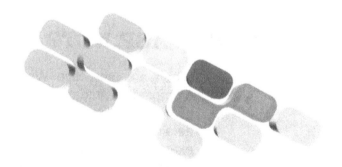

Introduction

Earlier versions of Visual Basic were excellent for creating applications which ran on a Windows PC, but increasingly there is a great demand for applications which run on the Web within a Web browser. Web pages originally consisted of simple HTML and were static, that is they allowed you to read information and to link to other pages, but that was all. The development of new technologies such as ASP (Active Server pages) and JSP (Java Server pages) allowed users to interact with Web pages, to produce the applications which are now common on the Web. In this chapter we are going to look at:

- What is ASP.NET?
- How to create Web applications.

In the next chapter we will look in more detail at the Web server controls.

What is ASP.NET?

When an interactive Web application runs, you are prompted for information, for example by selecting an item from a list or typing in your name or credit card details. This information is sent to the server, which examines the information you have supplied, perhaps references a database and then creates an HTML page which is sent back to you. The server may also send some DHTML (Dynamic HTML) back which contains an application which runs locally on your computer without the need to refer back to the server.

One of the methods of creating dynamic interactive Web pages is to use ASP. Visual Basic .NET uses Microsoft's extended version of ASP called ASP.NET.

ASP.NET has some important advantages over ASP, in particular:

- The Visual Basic .NET framework provides an excellent interactive user interface for rapid application development and debugging.
- ASP uses interpreted languages such a VBScript. ASP.NET uses fully compiled Visual Basic .NET which executes much faster.
- ASP.NET has a far more extensive set of controls, in particular server-side controls.

Before we look at how to develop Web applications we need consider some of the differences compared to Windows based applications.

Windows and Web applications

Many of the techniques used to develop Windows applications can be used for developing Web applications, however there are some important differences:

- You know far less about the environment in which the application is running when writing a Web application compared to a Windows application.
- The majority of the code for Web applications is on the Web server rather than the computer which is used to view the application.
- The time taken to respond to events will be far longer in Web applications because of the time taken to communicate with the server. This may not be significant, however if a server is being heavily used, it may be sufficient for users to notice that there is a delay. You should bear this in mind when developing Web applications and minimize the interactivity.
- Animations may not be satisfactory because of the need to refer to the server, but this can be

overcome to some extent by using DHTML which runs on the local machine.

- Different browsers have different capabilities and this may cause problems particularly with a new product such as this. If you are developing a commercial application you should ensure that your applications run satisfactorily with the most popular browsers.

These problems are not insignificant, however there is one major advantage to developing Web based applications. If you are developing commercial applications, it is easy to update the application – you just change the single copy on the server and it is automatically available to all users. This can be a huge saving in cost if the application has many users since updated versions and bug-fixes do not need to be sent to every customer.

What do I need to develop Web applications?

If you want to develop Web applications you need a Web server that supports ASP.NET such as IIS (Internet Information Server), with the required extensions installed. IIS is supplied with Windows 2000 Server and Windows XP Pro (but not the home edition).

Earlier versions of Windows such as 98 and ME support PWS (Personal Web Server), but are not suitable for creating and deploying Web applications.

Creating a Web application

To create a Web project select the **File | New | Project** menu option as shown in Figure 10.1.

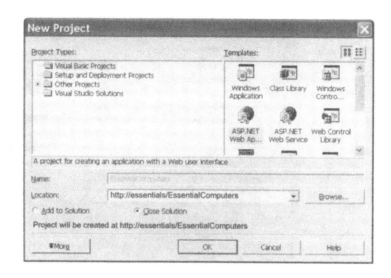

Figure 10.1 *Creating a Web application.*

You must specify the name of the application, *EssentialComputers* and the server it is to be created on, in this case a local server called *essentials*. You will need to supply the name of your own server. Click the **OK** button.

The running application we are going to develop is shown in Figure 10.2.

It has an **Image** control which provides the graphic at the top of the screen and a combination of controls which allow you to choose from a number of options and so specify the configuration of a computer you may wish to buy. When you click on the *OK* button, a summary of the items you have selected is displayed.

Most of the elements of creating a Web application are very similar to those used for Windows controls, however there are some important differences therefore we are going to look in detail at every stage of creating this application.

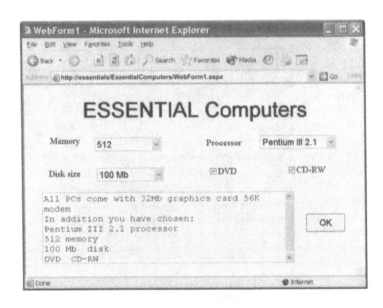

Figure 10.2 The running application.

Creating the application

After creating your Web application, the Solution Explorer should be similar to that shown in Figure 10.3. To display the design form double click on the default name of the Web form *WebForm1.aspx*

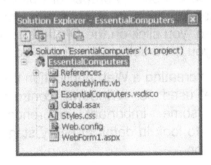

Figure 10.3 The Solution Explorer.

The controls are added in the same way as for a Windows application, but note that the toolbox provides a different page of controls specifically for Web applications.

- Add an **Image** control to the Form and change its **ImageURL** property to point to the graphic you wish to display.
- Add the **Label** controls and change their **Text** properties to *Memory, Processor* and *Disk size* as appropriate.
- Add the three **DropDownList** controls and change their names to *lstMemory, lstprocessor* and *lstDiskSize* as appropriate.
- Add the two **CheckBox** controls and change their **Text** properties to *DVD* and *CD RW* and their names to *chkDVD* and *chkCDRW*.
- Add the **TextBox** control and change its **Text** property to be blank and its name to *txtSummary*. Change the **TextMode** property to **MultiLine**.
- Add the **Button** and change its **Text** property to **OK** and its name to *btnOK*.
- Set the background colour of the form to an attractive colour using the **bgColor** property of the form.

The next is to add the list items to the **ListBox** controls. This is done by selecting each of these controls in turn and clicking on the button at the right of the **Items** property to display the ListItem Collection Editor as shown in Figure 10.4.

List items are added or deleted using this dialog by clicking the **Add** or **Remove** buttons. Any member can be edited by selecting it, and the position of a selected item can be changed by clicking on the arrowed keys on the right of the **Members** list.

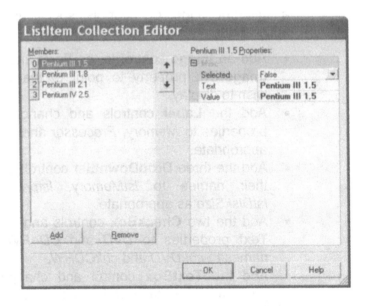

Figure 10.4 *The ListItem Collection Editor.*

The list items for the *Memory* **ListBox** are *256, 512* and *1024*. The *Disk size* **ListBox** has items *20Mb, 40Mb, 60Mb, 100Mb, 150Mb* and the *Processor* **ListBox** has items *Pentium III 1.5, Pentium III 1.8, Pentium 2.1* and *Pentium IV 2.5*.

It is a good idea to complete the user interface by fine tuning the position of the controls to exactly where you want them to be and altering the size of the font for these controls to provide an attractive appearance. The font can be changed by using the **Font | Size** property of the controls. Unlike Windows applications which allow you to choose a specific point size for the font you are limited to a range of textual options: **Smaller, Larger, XX Small, X Small, Small, Medium, Large, X Large** and **XX Large**. In the application shown here **Medium** was chosen for all controls.

At this stage the completed design form should appear similar to that shown in Figure 10.5.

Figure 10.5 The design form.

It is a good idea to run the application at this stage to make sure that the user interface has the appearance you want. The lists will be functional, but clicking on the **OK** button will not take any action.

As you add controls to the form and change the properties of controls, Visual Basic .NET converts this to HTML. If you click on the HTML tag at the bottom of the design window you can examine the code which has been generated. It is not advisable to change this unless you are expert at HTML. In practice it is not necessary since you can make all changes indirectly from the design form.

The final stage is to write the code which collects information on the items selected and displays them in the **TextBox** control.

The supporting code

As for Windows applications there is an event handler for dealing with the clicking of the *OK* button. To create an outline event handler double click on the *OK* button. If you need to create other event handlers for any event and control, you do so in exactly the same way as for Windows applications as shown in Figure 10.6.

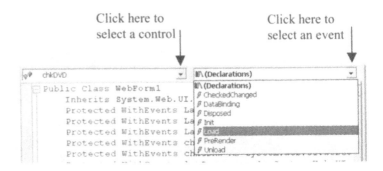

Click here to select a control |

Click here to select an event |

Figure 10.6 *Creating event handlers.*

The code for the event handler for the *OK* button is shown below:

```
Private Sub btnOK_Click(ByVal sender As System.Object, _
ByVal e As System.EventArgs) Handles btnOK.Click
Dim strSummary As String = "All PCs come with 32Mb graphics card"
    strSummary = strSummary & " 56K modem" & vbCrLf
    strSummary = strSummary & "In addition you have chosen: " _
        & vbCrLf
    strSummary = strSummary & lstProcessor.SelectedItem.Text & _
        " processor" & vbCrLf
    strSummary = strSummary & lstMemory.SelectedItem.Text & _
        " memory" & vbCrLf
    strSummary = strSummary & lstDiskSize.SelectedItem.Text & _
        " disk" & vbCrLf
    If chkDVD.Checked = True Then strSummary = strSummary & _
        "DVD "
    If chkCDRW.Checked = True Then strSummary = strSummary & _
        " CD-RW"
    txtSummary.Text = strSummary
End Sub
```

A **String** called *strSummary* is defined and is built up depending on which items have been chosen. This string is assigned to the **Text** property of the **TextBox** for display. The **vbCrLf** constant ensures that following text is placed on the next line. The item chosen from a **ListBox** is given by the **SelectedItem.Text** property. The state of the two **CheckBox** controls is given by examining the **Checked** property which is **True** if the box is checked (that is if the item has been chosen). This completes the application.

In the next chapter we are going to look at some more of the Web controls.

Chapter 11

Web Server Controls

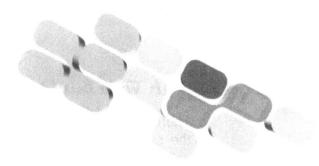

Introduction

We have seen how to create interactive Web applications and a few of the Web controls. In this chapter we are going to look at some further Web controls. Most of them are quite similar to the controls used for creating Windows applications, but there are some surprises caused by the limitations and characteristics of running in a browser environment. In this chapter we are going to look at:

- Some essential Web controls.
- How to use the Web controls.

Web controls

Visual Basic .NET offers a powerful set of controls for creating Web applications, most are very similar to their Windows counterparts, so we are going to concentrate on the differences between the two groups.

The Button Web controls

There are three types of **Button** Web server controls, the standard button which we have already seen in action.

The **LinkButton** looks like a standard hyperlink but behaves like a button. The text it displays is set using the **Text** property. If you want to create a link to a Web page use the **HyperLink** control.

The **ImageButton** allows you use a graphic as a button. You can choose the image by setting the **ImageURL** property. The three buttons are shown in Figure 11.1.

Figure 11.1 *The **Button** controls.*

One useful feature of the **ImageButton** is that not only can you tell when it has been clicked by using its **Click** event handler, you can tell where on the image it has been clicked, as shown in the event handler below which displays the X, Y co-ordinates on the position in a **Label** control called *lblShowPosition*.

```
Private Sub ImageButton1_Click(ByVal sender As System.Object, ByVal e _
    As System.Web.UI.ImageClickEventArgs) Handles ImageButton1.Click
        lblShowPosition.Text = e.X.ToString & " " & e.Y.ToString
End Sub
```

The Calendar control

The **Calendar** control is a useful and easy to use control which displays a one month calendar and built in navigation controls to allow you to move from one month to another.

≤	October 2002					≥
Mon	Tue	Wed	Thu	Fri	Sat	Sun
30	1	2	3	4	5	6
7	8	9	10	11	12	13
14	15	16	17	18	19	20
21	22	23	24	25	26	27
28	29	30	31	1	2	3
4	5	6	7	8	9	10

Figure 11.2 *The **Calendar** control.*

You can customize the appearance as shown in Figure 11.2, using the following properties : **DayHeaderStyle**, **NextPrevStyle**, **TodayDayStyle**, **OtherMonthStyle**,

SelectedDayStyle, **TitleStyle**, **WeekendDayStyle** and **DayStyle**.

The date which has been selected is available in the **SelectedDate** property, you can display the entire date using the **ToString** method or just parts of it using the **Day**, **Month** and **Year** properties. For example:

```
LblMonth.Text = CalCalendar.SelectedDate.Month.ToString
```

This displays the month containing the selected date in a **Label** control.

If you wish you can allow either a single day, a week or an entire month to be selected, or even disable selection using the **SelectionMode** property.

The CheckBox and CheckBoxList controls

The **CheckBox** control consists of a line of text and a box which can be unchecked or checked. The status of the control is given by the **Checked** property which is **True** if it is checked. When the control changes status the Web server is normally not informed of this – so the **CheckedChanged** event handler is not executed. It is more usual to check the status when a button is pressed to indicate that the required choices have been made on the form. If you wish the server to be informed every time the **CheckBox** is checked or unchecked, the **AutoPostBack** property must be set to **True**. If this is done the **CheckedChanged** event handler is run every time a change occurs.

If you want to have more than one **CheckBox** you can use a **CheckBoxList**, which is really a group of **CheckBox** controls. The items displayed are controlled by the **Items** property, for every line listed a new **CheckBox** is displayed. The spacing and alignment of the controls is handled automatically. Since more than one item may be checked in a

CheckBoxList you need to check the status of every **CheckBox** to determine which ones have been selected, that is have been checked. When a status change occurs in a **CheckBoxList** the **SelectedIndexChanged** event handler is called.

The next application shown in Figure 11.3 has a single **CheckBox** and a **CheckBoxList**. The **CheckBoxList** has a black border around it. The two **Label** controls indicate which **CheckBox** controls have been selected.

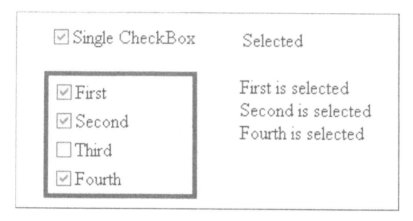

Figure 11.3 *The CheckBox and CheckBoxList controls.*

To create this application:

- Start a new Web project.
- Add the **CheckBox** control to the Web form, change its name to *chkCheckBox* and its **Text** property to *Single CheckBox*.
- Add a **CheckBoxList** and change its name to *chkCheckBoxList*.
- Add the two **Label** controls called *lblCheckBox* and *lblCheckBoxList*.
- The items listed in the **CheckBoxList** are set using the **Items** property.
- Finally since we want to display the changes every time a **CheckBox** changes its status, set the **AutoPostBack** properties of both the **CheckBox** and the **CheckBoxList** control to **True**.

The completed code for the application is shown below:

```
Private Sub chkCheckBoxList_SelectedIndexChanged(ByVal sender As _
    System.Object, ByVal e As System.EventArgs) Handles _
    chkCheckBoxList.SelectedIndexChanged
    Dim strStatus As String
    Dim lst As ListItem
    strStatus = ""
    For Each lst In chkCheckBoxList.Items
        If lst.Selected = True Then
            strStatus = strStatus & vbCrLf & lst.Text & " is selected"
        End If
    Next
    lblCheckBoxList.Text = strStatus
End Sub

Private Sub chkCheckBox_CheckedChanged(ByVal sender As System.Object, _
ByVal e As System.EventArgs) Handles chkCheckBox.CheckedChanged
    If chkCheckBox.Checked = True Then
        lblCheckBox.Text = "Selected"
    Else
        lblCheckBox.Text = "Not selected"
    End If
End Sub
```

Note the use of the **For Each..Next** statement.

The DropDownList control

We have already seen the **DropDownList** control in action. The key functional difference between a **DropDownList** control and a **ListBox** control is that a **DropDownList** only allows you to select a single item unlike a **ListBox** which allows you to select one or more items.

The HyperLink control

The **HyperLink** control is used to provide a standard hyperlink. The address to link to is specified in the **NavigateURL** property. The text which is displayed is determined by the **Text** property, however if you wish you can display an image instead by using the **ImageURL** property. If you do display an image as well as text the image is displayed and the text is shown when the cursor hovers over it.

The Image control

We have already seen the **Image** control which is used to display an image on a Web page. If the image is not available, the text specified by the **AlternateText** property is displayed.

The Label control

We have also seen the **Label** control already. It is used to display text (specified in the **Text** property) which the viewer cannot change.

The ListBox control

The **ListBox** control displays a list of items and allows one or more to be selected.

The entries in the list are specified in the **Items** property. If the **ListBox** is not sufficiently large to display all of the items a vertical scroll bar is automatically added.

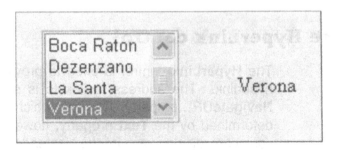

Figure 11.4 *The **ListBox** control.*

Figure 11.4 shows a **ListBox** control with a **Label** alongside indicating which item has been selected.

The event handler for the **SelectedIndexChanged** event is shown below. The name of the **ListBox** is *lstHoliday* and the name of the **Label** is *lblHoliday*.

```
Private Sub lstHoliday_SelectedIndexChanged(ByVal sender _
   As System.Object, ByVal e As System.EventArgs) _
   Handles lstHoliday.SelectedIndexChanged
      If lstHoliday.SelectedIndex = -1 Then
            lblHoliday.Text = "None"
      Else
            lblHoliday.Text = lstHoliday.SelectedItem.Text
      End If
End Sub
```

When no item has been selected, the **SelectedIndex** property is −1. The **AutoPostBack** property of the **ListBox** must be set to **True** for the server to be informed of new selections, and therefore the event handler executed.

If you set the **SelectionMode** property from the default of **Single** to **Multiple**, more than one item may be selected. If you try to use the **SelectedItem** property to identify which option has been selected only the first in the list to be selected is reported. To identify all items you must check each one in turn using the same technique as used for the **CheckBoxList** control.

The Panel control

The **Panel** control provides a container for other controls. The benefits of this are that the **Panel** and the controls it contains can be given a custom appearance and hidden and displayed as a group.

The RadioButton and RadioButtonList controls

The **RadioButton** and **RadioButtonList** are similar to the **CheckBox** and **CheckBoxList** controls, the principal difference is that **RadioButtons** are grouped and only one **RadioButton** in that group can be selected at a time. Selecting a **RadioButton** automatically deselects the others in that group.

If you wish to use individual **RadioButtons**, you can group them by giving them the same **GroupName** property value. The text which is displayed is determined by the **Text** property and the position of the button relative to the text is controlled by the **TextAlign** property. In Figure 11.5 the left column of **RadioButton** controls have a **TextAlign** property set to **Left**.

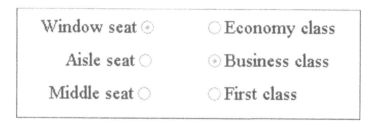

Figure 11.5 The *RadioButton* controls.

The **RadioButtonList** control embodies a set of **RadioButton** controls in the same way as the **CheckBoxList** controls embodies a set of **CheckBox** controls, and the behaviour of the two pairs of controls is similar.

When a single **RadioButton** is selected the **CheckedChanged** event occurs. When a **RadioButton** in a **RadioButtonList** is selected the **SelectedIndexChanged** event occurs.

When these events occur for both **RadioButton** and **RadioButtonList** controls the server is not informed unless the **AutoPostBack** property is set to **True**.

Chapter 12

Working with Forms

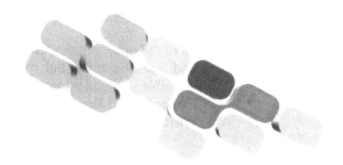

Introduction

Forms are graphical objects, which must be instantiated like any other object. A form object is a window or dialog which acts as a container for controls. Forms also have their own set of properties and methods. In this chapter we are going to look at how you can use these properties and methods to create the sort of applications you want. Dialogs are a special type of window which are used for displaying messages. In this chapter we are going to look at using forms in Windows applications, in particular:

- Creating new forms.
- Showing and hiding forms.
- Controlling form properties and position.
- MDI forms.
- Adding menus to forms.

Adding new forms

All of the applications that we have created so far have had just one form, but most applications need more than this. To add a form to your application choose the **Project | Add New Items** menu option and choose the **Windows Forms** option as shown in Figure 12.1.

The startup form

The form which is displayed when the application starts is the form which is initially created when you start the application, however you can change this:

- Select the project in the Solution Explorer.
- Right click and select the **Properties** menu option.

- On the **General** page select the form which you want the project to start with.

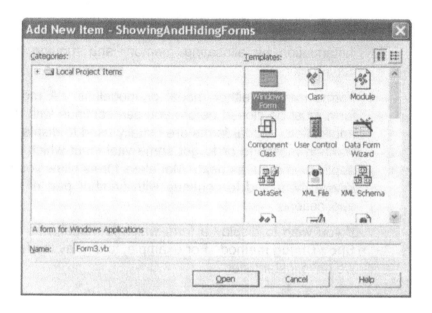

Figure 12.1 Adding a new Form.

Creating forms

An instance of the startup form is created and displayed at run-time. If you want to use other form objects you must instantiate them at run-time. For example to instantiate a form called *frmSplash*:

```
Dim frmSplash As New Form( )
```

frmSplash is an instance of the standard empty **Form** class, but if you wish you can create a sub-class of **Form** at either design-time or run-time which may contain a set of controls and create a new instance of this, as we show in the next application.

The instantiation may be broken into two stages:

```
Dim frmSplash As Form
frmSplash = new Form( )
```

the first line declaring *frmSplash* as a member of the **Form** class and the second performing the instantiation by allocating memory and running the constructor.

Forms may be either modal or modeless. A modal form must be closed before you can continue with the application. Modal forms are usually used to display a warning message or to get some vital input which the application requires next. Modeless forms allow you to ignore them and to continue with another part of the application.

If you wish to display a form which is modal, use the **ShowDialog** method. For example, to display the form we have instantiated:

```
frmSplash.ShowDialog( )
```

To display the same form as a modeless dialog use the **Show** method:

```
frmSplash.Show( )
```

To hide this form the **Hide** method is used:

```
frmSplash.Hide( )
```

There is no longer a **Load** method in Visual Basic, memory space and resources are allocated for a form object when it is instantiated.

Hiding and showing forms

In the next application we are going to create an application which creates an instance of a form and displays it. When the *Create new Form* **Button** is clicked, a second form is created as shown in Figure 12.2. Clicking on the *Dispose* button on either of the forms removes the second form.   The first form is called *FrmStartup*, the second form is called *frm2*.

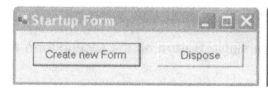 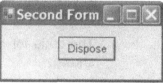

Figure 12.2 *The running application.*

To create this application:

- Start a Windows project.
- Change the name of the default form created from *Form1* to *FrmStartup*.
- Add the title and the two **Button** controls as shown on the left of Figure 12.2.
- Select the **Project | Add New Items | Windows Forms** menu option to create the second form.
- Change the name of the second form to *frm2*.
- Add the title and **Button** control as shown on the right of Figure 12.2.

The startup form, shown on the left of figure 12.2, has two buttons, *btnCreate* and *btnDispose*. Their event procedures are shown below:

```
Public Class FrmStartup
    Inherits System.Windows.Forms.Form
    Dim frmSecond As frm2
    Private Sub btnCreate_Click(ByVal sender As System.Object, _
    ByVal e As System.EventArgs) Handles btnCreate.Click
        frmSecond = New frm2( )
        frmSecond.Show( )
    End Sub

    Private Sub BtnDispose_Click(ByVal sender As System.Object, _
    ByVal e As System.EventArgs) Handles btnDispose.Click
        frmSecond.Dispose( )
    End Sub
End Class
```

Note the **Dim** statement, which declares that *frmSecond* is a member of the *frm2* class, is outside of any procedure and is therefore available for use within any procedure in this class.

The code for the single **Button** on the second form is shown:

```
Private Sub btnDispose_Click(ByVal sender As System.Object, _
ByVal e As System.EventArgs) Handles btnDispose.Click
    Me.Dispose( )
End Sub
```

Note the use of **Me**, to refer to the current object, that is the second form in this case, since the procedure is for a control on that form.

However, this application has some unwanted behaviour.

- If you click on the *Dispose* button on the first form before creating a second form, the application crashes and an error message is displayed which indicates that an exception has occurred: **System.NullReferenceException**. This is caused by attempting to dispose of an object which has not yet been created.
- The second problem is that you can create as many new forms as you wish by repeatedly clicking on the **Create new Form** button. When you have created more than one copy of the second form, the *Dispose* button on the first form only deletes the last one to be created, however you can delete each form in turn by clicking on its *Delete* button.

The easiest way to fix both of these problems is to check to see if the second form already exists. If it does not, no attempt should be made to dispose of it. If it does exist, a further form should not be created. These changes prevent the application from crashing. The new version of the event procedure for the startup form is:

```
Private Sub btnCreate_Click(ByVal sender As System.Object, _
ByVal e As System.EventArgs) Handles btnCreate.Click
    If Not frmSecond Is Nothing Then frmSecond.Dispose( )
    frmSecond = New frm2( )
    frmSecond.Show( )
End Sub

Private Sub BtnDispose_Click(ByVal sender As System.Object, _
ByVal e As System.EventArgs) Handles btnDispose.Click
    If Not frmSecond Is Nothing Then frmSecond.Dispose( )
    frmSecond.Dispose( )
End Sub
```

A single line has been added to each event handler to see if *frmSecond* has been instantiated, if it has then it is disposed of.

The second form does not require any changes.

Controlling form properties

Forms have an extensive set of properties, however the ones which are most often changed from their defaults are the **Name**, **Text**, **BackColor**, **BackgroundImage** and the **FormBorderStyle** properties. **Name** has no visual aspect, but the other properties greatly affect the appearance of the form.

The **Name** property is used to refer to the form.

The **Text** property is displayed on the title bar at the top of the form. This should be changed to some text which will help the user of the program to know what the function of the form is.

The **BackColor** property determines the colour of the form. You can choose a colour which is the same as one of the System colours, for example, the colour of an Active Border as specified in your Windows setup. Alternatively, you can choose any colour from a palette.

The **BackgroundImage** property allows an image to be displayed on the form, any controls added will appear on top of this image. If the image is smaller than the form, the image is tiled to cover the entire area. To remove the background picture completely right click on the property in the Properties Window and select the **Reset** option.

The **FormBorderStyle** property has seven possible settings:

- **None**. The form has no border.
- **FixedSingle**. A fixed single border, resizable only using the maximize and minimize buttons.
- **Fixed3D**. A fixed size dialog with a 3D look.
- **FixedDialog**. A fixed size dialog box, without maximize or minimize buttons.
- **FixedToolWindow**. A fixed size window. It has a close button and the title is displayed in a small font size.
- **Sizable**. The default. The border has minimize and maximize buttons. It is resizable.
- **SizableToolWindow**. A resizable window. It has a close button and the title is displayed in a small font size.

You can change this at design-time using the Properties window or you can do it in code, for example, to give the current Form(referred to as **Me**) a **Fixed3D** border:

```
Me.FormBorderStyle = FormBorderStyle.Fixed3D
```

For some applications you may wish to prevent the window being minimized or maximized, you can do this by using the **MinimizeBox** and **MaximizeBox** properties:

- If **MinimizeBox** is set to **True** the form has a minimize button.
- If **MaximizeButton** is set **True** the form has a maximize button.

- If the **FormBorderStyle** property is either **None, FixedToolWindow** or **SizableToolWindow** these properties have no effect.

Control the Window position

If your application always uses maximized windows you do not have to worry about where the window is positioned on the screen, however if this is not the case you may want to specify this explicitly rather than relying on defaults.

The form position when it is loaded is determined by the **StartPosition** property, the default for this property is **WindowsDefaultLocation**, which is a position calculated by the operating system to be suitable for the form. The **CenterScreen** option is a more predictable option to use. If you want to have more control over the position, set this property to **Manual** and specify the position using the **Location** property. You can change this property at design-time or programmatically, for example:

```
Me.Location = New Point(400, 400)
```

This changes the position to 400,400. The top left corner of the screen is the 0,0 position.

If you wish you can change the X and Y co-ordinates separately using the **Left** and **Top** properties, for example:

```
Me.Left = 200
Me.Top = 300
```

You can also move the form to a position relative to its current position, for example:

```
Me.Left += 20
Me.Top += 30
```

This moves the form 20 pixels right and 30 pixels lower relative to its current position.

MDI forms

MDI or Multiple Document Interface forms consist of child forms contained within a parent form. Figure 12.3 shows an MDI parent form with three child forms.

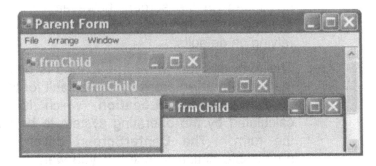

Figure 12.3 *Parent and child forms.*

At run-time, all child forms are displayed within the MDI form, but they can be moved and sized within this area as normal.   Both child and parent forms can be minimized, but when a parent form is minimized, it and all the child forms it contains are represented by a single icon.

To illustrate the use of MDI forms and also how to use the menu system we are going to look at an application which allows you to create as many child windows as you wish and to view and order them.

Creating an MDI application

To create an MDI application:

- Start a Windows project by selecting the **File | New Project** menu option and choosing **Windows Application** from the types of project available.
- Change the **Text** property of the form to *Parent Form* and the name property to *frmParent*.
- Set the **IsMdiContainer** property to **True**.
- Create a child form class by selecting the **Project | Add Windows Form** menu item and selecting the **Windows Form** option. Name this form class *frmChild*.

The next stage is to add the menu system.

Creating the menu system

To create a menu add a **MainMenu** control from the toolbox to the form. Your form in the design window will appear as shown in Figure 12.4.

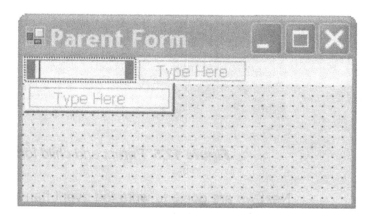

Figure 12.4 *Creating a menu system.*

The menu system we are going to create has the following entries:

- A *File* heading which contains 2 items: *New child* and *Close*.

- An *Arrange* heading which contains 3 items: *Cascade*, *Tile horizontal* and *Tile vertical*.
- A *Window* heading which contains no items: but will display a list of all the child windows.

The completed menu system is shown in Figure 12.5.

Note that the line between the *New child* and *Close* options was inserted by adding a single dash as one of the menu items, this is converted to an unbroken line.

The name of all menu items is be changed to have the prefix *mnu* followed by the text of the menu item, for example *mnuClose*.

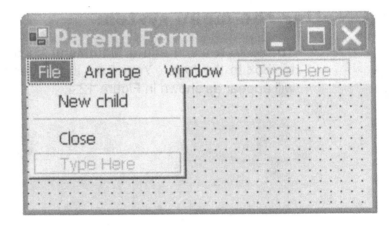

Figure 12.5 *Parent and child forms.*

Next we are going to write the event handlers for each of these menu items.

Menu event procedures

To create the event procedures double click on the menu item. The code for the *File | New child* menu item is shown below.

```
Private Sub MnuNewChild_Click(ByVal sender As System.Object, _
  ByVal e As System.EventArgs) Handles MnuNewChild.Click
    Dim newChildForm As New frmChild( )
    newChildForm.MdiParent = Me
    newChildForm.Show( )
End Sub
```

A new instance of the child form *frmChild* is created by the **Dim** statement. The parent of the child form is designated as the current MDI parent form. Finally the child form is displayed by the **Show** method.

If you want you can run the application at this stage: a new child form will be displayed every time you select this menu option.

The *File | Close* menu option consists of one line:

```
Me.Dispose( )
```

which closes the application.

The code for the *Arrange | Cascade* menu item consists of a single line:

```
Me.LayoutMdi(System.Windows.Forms.MdiLayout.Cascade)
```

Similarly for the *Arrange | Tile horizontal* menu option:

```
Me.LayoutMdi(System.Windows.Forms.MdiLayout.TileHorizontal)
```

and for the *Arrange |Tile vertical* menu option:

```
Me.LayoutMdi(System.Windows.Forms.MdiLayout.TileVertical)
```

For the *Windows* menu option, there are no sub-items or code required, just select it and change the **MdiList** property to **True**. When this item is selected a list of the current child windows is displayed.

The running application is shown in Figure 12.6, with horizontally tiled child forms and the *File* menu expanded.

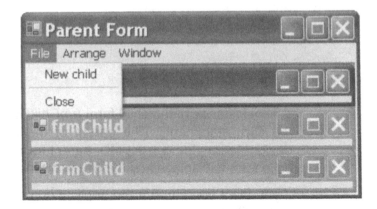

Figure 12.6 *The running application.*

Chapter 13

Working with Dialogs

Introduction

We have already looked at how to create Windows applications which use forms. In this chapter we are going to look at a special type of form called a dialog. A dialog is normally a modal form which waits for user input and does not allow the application to proceed until it is closed. The **MessageBox** class is a pre-defined dialog box which can be used for common operations. In addition there are a set of standard dialogs which carry out common operations such as selecting a file or a colour. In this chapter we are going to look at:

- The **MessageBox** class
- The **InputBox** function.
- Some standard Windows dialogs.

The MessageBox class

The **MsgBox** function is still supported, and may be used, but the use of the **MessageBox** class is the preferred way of displaying dialogs. There is no guarantee that the **MsgBox** function will be supported in later versions.

To display a dialog the **Show** method is used. There are numerous overloaded methods. The parameters for the most common form are:

- The text displayed on the dialog.
- The text displayed on the heading.
- The buttons which can be displayed. There are six combinations of **Abort**, **Retry**, **Ignore**, **OK** and **Cancel** buttons which can be displayed from the **MessageBoxButtons** enumeration.

- An optional parameter which identifies the icon which is displayed, using the **MessageBoxIcon** enumeration.

An example of using the **Show** method of the **MessageBox** class is shown below:

```
MessageBox.Show("Are you sure?", "Holiday booking", _
MessageBoxButtons.YesNoCancel, MessageBoxIcon.Exclamation)
```

This code displays the dialog shown in Figure 13.1.

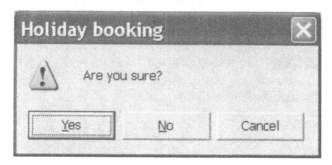

Figure 13.1 *Using the **MessageBox** class.*

The eight members of the **MessageBoxIcon** enumeration:

- Asterisk.
- Error.
- Exclamation.
- Hand.
- Information.
- Question.
- Stop.
- Warning.

Figure 13.1 uses the Exclamation icon. The icon which is displayed is a function of the operating system and currently some of the members show the same symbol: Asterisk and Information; Error, Hand and Stop; Exclamation and Warning. Only the Question icon is unique. This is likely to change in later versions of the operating system.

Which button was pressed?

In addition to displaying a message you need to receive input from the **MessageBox**, that is, to know which button has been pressed.

The result can be tested against a set of pre-defined values defined in the **DialogResult** enumeration, for example **DialogResult.OK** is returned if the *OK* button has been pressed. In the example below, if the *Yes* button has been pressed the application ends.

```
If MessageBox.Show("Are you sure", "Exit Application", _
MessageBoxButtons.YesNoCancel, MessageBoxIcon.Question) _
    = DialogResult.Yes Then
    Application.Exit( )
    End If
```

The InputBox function

If you want to use a dialog to input some text the **InputBox** function can be used. The general form is:

```
Result = InputBox (prompt, title, defaultResponse, xpos, ypos)
```

- *Result* is the text which is typed into the **InputBox**.
- *prompt* is the string that is displayed in the dialog box.
- *title* is the title in the dialog box's title bar.
- *defaultResponse:* optional, the initial text placed in the **TextBox**. If you omit this parameter the **TextBox** is blank.
- *xpos:* optional, is the distance from the left edge of the screen to the dialog box. If you omit this parameter the dialog is centred horizontally.
- *ypos:* optional, is the distance from the top of the screen to the top of the dialog box. If you omit this

parameter, the dialog is positioned vertically about a third of the way down the screen.

InputBox always has the buttons **OK** and **Cancel**. The dialog box produced by the code below is shown in Figure 13.2.

```
Dim strPrompt As String, strTitle As String
Dim strDefault As String, strName As String
strPrompt = "Who are you?"
strTitle = "Athens database search"
strDefault = "John Cowell"
strName = InputBox(strPrompt, strTitle, strDefault)
```

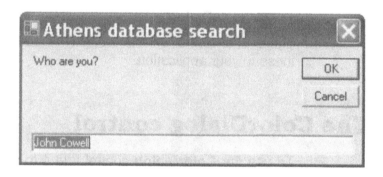

*Figure 13.2 Using **InputBox**.*

Missing optional parameters

A common problem occurs when you want to miss an optional parameter from a list. If the parameter is the last in the list you can simply omit it. The difficulty arises when you want to miss a parameter but include one that comes after it. If, for example, you wish to specify the y position of an input box, but not the x position. You do this by omitting the *xpos* parameter but including the comma separator before the *ypos* parameter, for example:

```
intResponse = InputBox("File name?", "File Input", "Project.txt", , ypos)
```

Standard Dialogs

All windows applications have a similar appearance – for example whenever you open or save a file, choose a colour, or a font – since Windows has a set of standard dialog boxes which carry out these operations. We are going to look at four of them:

- **ColorDialog**.
- **FontDialog**.
- **OpenFileDialog**.
- **SaveFileDialog**.

There is a control on the toolbox for adding each of these to your application.

The ColorDialog control

To use the **ColorDialog** control add it to your form in the usual way. Figure 13.3 shows the expanded form of the dialog with the custom colours. Clicking on the question mark on the top right of the dialog and clicking elsewhere, a help message is displayed, as shown.

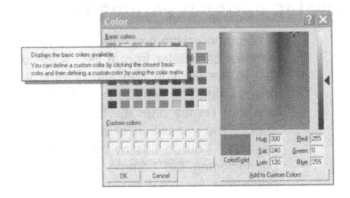

*Figure 13.3 The **ColorDialog** control.*

The dialog is displayed using the **ShowDialog** method.

To specify that the custom colours may be displayed, the **AllowFullOpen** property is set to **True**. You can also add a help button to the dialog by setting the **ShowHelp** property to **True**.

The code below displays the dialog shown in Figure 13.3 and assigns the colour returned in the **Color** property of the dialog to the **ForeColor** of the current form.

```
dlgColour.ShowHelp = False        ' do not show help button
dlgColour.AllowFullOpen = True    ' allow custom colours to be displayed
dlgColour.ShowDialog( )           ' show the dialog
Me.ForeColor = dlgColour.Color    ' change the foreColor of the form.
```

The FontDialog Control

The **FontDialog** control in action is shown in Figure 13.4. This familiar dialog allows you to select a font, font style, and size.

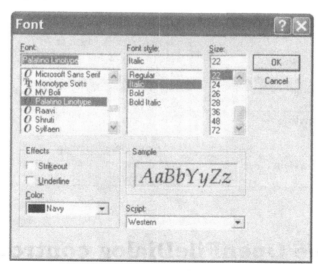

Figure 13.4 The FontDialog control.

If you also wish to be able to choose the colour of the font the **ShowColor** property must be set to **True** and assigned to the **ForeColor** property of the **Font** property of the **TextBox** as shown in the code below:

```
dlgFont.ShowColor = True
dlgFont.ShowDialog( )
txtChameleon.Font = dlgFont.Font
txtChameleon.ForeColor = dlgFont.Color
```

The **FontDialog** control is called *dlgFont* and *txtChameleon* is a **TextBox** whose text is changed to reflect the changes in font, style, size and colour as selected.

Other often used properties of this control are shown in Table 13.1.

Table 13.1 Common properties of the **FontDialog** Control.

Property	Description
AllowVectorFonts	Sets or returns a value indicating if vector fonts are displayed in the dialog.
FixedPitchOnly	Sets or returns a value indicating if only fixed-pitch fonts are displayed in the dialog.
FontMustExist	Sets or returns a value which determines if an error message is displayed if a font or style which does not exist is selected.
MaxSize	Sets or returns the maximum font size which can be selected.
MinSize	Sets or returns the minimum font size which can be selected.
ShowEffects	Sets or returns a value which indicates if the dialog displays options for setting underline, strikethrough and colour.
ShowHelp	Sets or returns a value which indicates if the dialog contains a help button.

The OpenFileDialog control

The **OpenFileDialog** control displays the standard Windows dialog used for selecting a file. This dialog in common with all of this set of standard dialogs is displayed using the **ShowDialog** method.

Figure 13.5 shows an application which displays pictures. Clicking on the **File | Open** menu option of the *Holiday Pictures* Form displays the **OpenFileDialog** and allows a file to be selected. The chosen file is displayed in the **PictureBox** control.

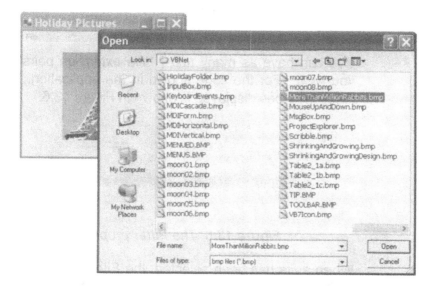

*Figure 13.5 The **OpenFileDialog** control.*

The **PictureBox** is called *picHoliday* and the **OpenFileDialog** control *dlgOpenFile*. The event procedure for the **File | Open** menu option is shown below:

```
Private Sub mnuOpen_Click(ByVal sender As System.Object, _
ByVal e As System.EventArgs) Handles mnuOpen.Click
   dlgOpenFile.InitialDirectory = "C:\"
   dlgOpenFile.Filter = _
   "bmp files (*.bmp)|*.bmp|jpg files(*.jpg)|*.jpg|gif files(*.gif)|*.gif|All files (*.*)|*.*"
   dlgOpenFile.ShowDialog( )
   picHoliday.Image = Image.FromFile(dlgOpenFile.FileName)
End Sub
```

The **InitialDirectory** property is used to determine which directory is displayed when the dialog is first displayed.

Since we want to open an image file, the **Filter** property is used to ensure that only files with an extension of bmp, jpg or gif are displayed in the dialog. The syntax used to set this property looks confusing at first. Its general form is:

```
"text | *.file extension | text | *.file extension"
```

You can have as many *text | *.file extension* pairs as you wish. For the code shown in the application, the list of file types displayed is shown in Figure 13.6.

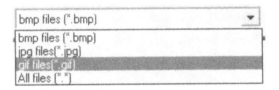

*Figure 13.6 The **Filter** property.*

When a file has been selected, the **Filename** property of the dialog is assigned the name of that file. This is a **String** and since the **Image** property of a **PictureBox** is an **Image** object, these two properties cannot be assigned to each other. The **Image.FromFile** method of the **Image** class returns an **Image** object which can be assigned to the **Image** property of the **PictureBox**.

If the **Cancel** button is pressed, the above application will fail with an **ArgumentException**, since an attempt is made to open a non-existent file. This can be handled by using a **Try Catch** clause as shown below around the line which sets the **Image** property of the **PictureBox.**

```
Try
    picHoliday.Image = Image.FromFile(dlgOpenFile.FileName)
Catch exnNoPicture As System.ArgumentException
End Try
```

In this case, no action is taken if the exception occurs, but you could, for example display a dialog asking the user to try again.

We have already looked at the many commonly used properties of this dialog, a few others are shown in Table 13.2.

Table 13.2 Common properties of the **OpenFileDialog** control.

Property	Description
FileName	Returns the name of the single file selected.
FileNames	Returns the file names of all selected files. Note the final s.
MultiSelect	Sets or returns whether selection of more than one file is allowed.
ReadOnlyChecked	Sets or returns whether read-only files are displayed.
ShowHelp	Sets or returns a value to determine whether the dialog displays a help button.

If you wish to return more than one item, set the **MultiSelect** property to **True**. The items selected are returned as an array of strings in the **FileNames** property. For example, a **String** array called *selectedFiles* can be declared:

```
Dim selectedFiles(10) As String
```

The filenames selected can be assigned to this array by the statement:

```
selectedFiles = dlgOpenFile.FileNames
```

The first file name selected is in the first element of the array, that is *selectedFiles(0)*, the second file name is in *selectedFiles(1)* and so on. The number of files chosen is given by *selectedFiles*.**Length**.

The SaveFileDialog Control

The **SaveFileDialog**, shown in Figure 13.7, is very similar in appearance and properties to the **OpenFileDialog**.

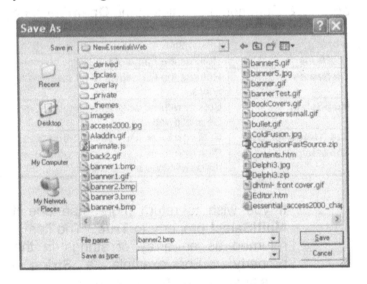

Figure 13.7 *The* **SaveFileDialog** *control.*

The **Overwrite** property returns or sets a value to indicate if a warning dialog is displayed if an existing file is to be over-written.

Chapter

14

Mouse and Keyboard Events

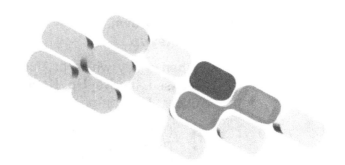

Introduction

When a mouse is moved or one of its buttons clicked an event happens, similarly when a button on the keyboard is pressed an event occurs. The processing of these events is an area in Visual Basic. In this chapter we are going to look at:

- The keyboard events.
- The mouse events.
- The mouse button events.
- Dragging and dropping objects.
- The effect of the Shift, Ctrl and Alt buttons on using the mouse.

Keyboard events

There are three keyboard events:

- **KeyPress**.
- **KeyDown**.
- **KeyUp**.

When a key which produces a printable character is pressed, the **KeyUp**, **KeyDown** and **KeyPress** events occur. For non-printable keys such as:

- The function keys.
- The navigation keys.
- The Shift key.

only **KeyUp** and **KeyDown** occur not **KeyPress**.

The header for the event handler for a **ListBox** control called *lstKeyEvents* when the **KeyDown** event occurs is shown below:

```
Private Sub lstKeyEvents_KeyDown(ByVal sender As Object, _
    ByVal e As System.Windows.Forms.KeyEventArgs) Handles _
    lstKeyEvents.KeyDown
```

The **KeyUp** event handler has the same pair of parameters. The **KeyEventArgs** object indicates which key was pressed and if any of the modifier keys (Ctrl, Shift and Alt) were also pressed.

The event handler for the **KeyPress** event is passed a **KeyPressEventArgs** object which specifies the character which is to be displayed, for example if the Shift and 'a' key are pressed, the character is an upper case A.

Monitoring keyboard events

The following simple application shows how the keyboard events can be used. In this application, the name of the event name is added to a **ListBox** control called *lstKeyEvents* whenever that event occurs by pressing any key on the keyboard:

```
Private Sub lstKeyEvents_KeyDown(ByVal sender As Object, _
   ByVal e As System.Windows.Forms.KeyEventArgs) Handles _
   lstKeyEvents.KeyDown
      lstKeyEvents.Items.Add("----------------")
' if ten or more items in the list box clear it
      If lstKeyEvents.Items.Count >= 10 Then lstKeyEvents.Items.Clear( )
      lstKeyEvents.Items.Add("KeyDown")
End Sub

Private Sub lstKeyEvents_KeyUp(ByVal sender As Object, _
   ByVal e As System.Windows.Forms.KeyEventArgs) Handles _
   lstKeyEvents.KeyUp
      lstKeyEvents.Items.Add("KeyUp")
End Sub

Private Sub lstKeyEvents_KeyPress(ByVal sender As Object, _
   ByVal e As System.Windows.Forms.KeyPressEventArgs) Handles _
   lstKeyEvents.KeyPress
      lstKeyEvents.Items.Add("KeyPress")
End Sub
```

The running application is shown in Figure 14.1, after two non-printable keys and a printable key have been pressed.

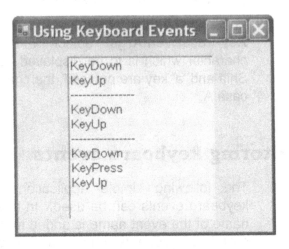

Figure 14.1 The keyboard events.

The modifier keys

The next application we are going to look at is shown running in Figure 14.2.

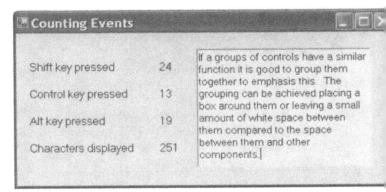

Figure 14.2 Counting keyboard events.

This application counts the number of times the Alt, Ctrl and Shift key are pressed and also the number of printable keys pressed (note that pressing the Delete key counts as one of this number).

The four labels which display the count are called *lblShift*, *lblCtrl*, *lblAlt* and *lblCharacterCount*. The **TextBox** control where the text is typed is called *txtInput*.

The event procedure for the **KeyPress** event is used to count the number of printable keys pressed. The string stored in the **Text** property of the **Label** which counts the number of characters is converted to an integer using the **Cint** method. It is incremented by 1 and then converted back to a string using the **CStr** method. The result is displayed in the **Label** control.

The event procedure for the **KeyDown** event is used to detect the state of the Shift, Ctrl and Alt keys, by looking at the **Shift**, **Alt** and **Control** properties of the **KeyEventArgs** object which is passed to event procedure.

The complete code for this application is shown below:

```
Private Sub txtInput_KeyPress(ByVal sender As Object, _
    ByVal e As System.Windows.Forms.KeyPressEventArgs) _
    Handles txtInput.KeyPress
        lblCharacterCount.Text = CStr(CInt(lblCharacterCount.Text) + 1)
End Sub

Private Sub txtInput_KeyDown(ByVal sender As Object, _
    ByVal e As System.Windows.Forms.KeyEventArgs) _
    Handles txtInput.KeyDown
        If e.Shift = True Then
            lblShift.Text = CStr(CInt(lblShift.Text) + 1)
        ElseIf e.Alt = True Then
            lblAlt.Text = CStr(CInt(lblAlt.Text) + 1)
        ElseIf e.Control = True Then
            lblCtrl.Text = CStr(CInt(lblCtrl.Text) + 1)
        End If
End Sub
```

Mouse events

We are going to look at five mouse events

- **MouseDown**.
- **MouseUp**.
- **MouseMove**.
- **MouseEnter**.
- **MouseLeave**.

MouseDown, MouseUp and MouseMove

The **MouseDown** and **MouseUp** events are caused when any of the mouse buttons is pressed and released. The **MouseMove** event occurs when the mouse moves. When these events occur an event handler is called, for example, if a **MouseUp** event occurs on a **PictureBox** control called *picLaSanta*:

```
Private Sub picLaSanta_MouseUp(ByVal sender As Object, _
    ByVal e As System.Windows.Forms.MouseEventArgs) _
    Handles picLaSanta.MouseUp

.....
End Sub
```

This procedure is passed two parameters which give us more information about the event which has occurred:

- The first parameter is an object which indicates where the event originated from.
- The second parameter is a **MouseEventArgs** object which gives information about the event which has occurred such as the co-ordinates of the position where the event happened.

We are going to look in more detail at the **MouseEventArgs** class.

The MouseEventArgs Class

MouseEventArgs objects have five properties:

- *Button* : This indicates which button was pressed. This may be one of five possible buttons: right, middle, left and also XButton1 and XButton2; the last two buttons are to provide support for the new Microsoft mouse called the IntelliMouse Explorer. The two additional buttons provide backward and forward navigation.
- *Clicks* : The number of times the mouse button was pressed and released.
- *Delta* : A signed number giving the number of detents or rotations of the mouse wheel.
- *X* : The x co-ordinates of the location where the event occurred.
- *Y* : The y co-ordinates of the location where the event occurred.

To illustrate how these events can be used, we are going to look at an application shown running in Figure 14.3.

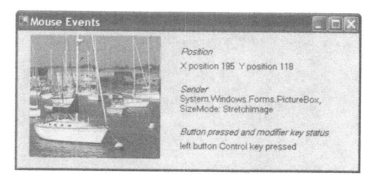

Figure 14.3 *The MouseUp, Down and Move events.*

An image is displayed in the **PictureBox** called *picLaSanta*, when the mouse is moved over the picture or a mouse button is pressed, the three **Label** controls on the right of the picture show:

- The position of the mouse when the event occurs.
- The originator of the event.
- The status of the mouse buttons and if one of the Alt, Ctrl or Shift keys has been pressed.

The event procedure for the **MouseDown** event for the **PictureBox** is shown below.

```
Private Sub picLaSanta_MouseDown(ByVal sender As Object, _
    ByVal e As System.Windows.Forms.MouseEventArgs) _
    Handles picLaSanta.MouseDown
        display(sender, e)
End Sub
```

In common with the event procedures for the **MouseUp** and **MouseMove** events it only contains one line, a call to another method called *display*. This has been done because the action taken is the same for every event. This method is passed the two parameters which are passed to all the event procedures and updates the text which is displayed in the three labels, *lblPosition*, *lblSender* and *lblModifierKey*. The complete application is shown below.

```
Private Sub display(ByVal sender As Object, _
    ByVal e As System.Windows.Forms.MouseEventArgs)
        Dim t As String
        lblPosition.Text = "X position " & CStr(e.X) & " Y position " & CStr(e.Y)
        lblSender.Text = sender.ToString( )
        If (e.Button = MouseButtons.Right) Then
                t = "right button"
        Elseif (e.Button = MouseButtons.Left) Then
                t = "left button"
        Elseif (e.Button = MouseButtons.Middle) Then
                t = "middle button"
        Elseif (e.Button = MouseButtons.XButton1) Then
                t = "XButton1"
```

```
        ElseIf (e.Button = MouseButtons.XButton2) Then
            t = "XButton2"
        Else : t = "none"
        End If
        If (Control.ModifierKeys And Keys.Shift) Then
            t = t & " Shift key pressed"
        ElseIf (Control.ModifierKeys And Keys.Control) Then
            t = t & " Control key pressed"
        ElseIf (Control.ModifierKeys And Keys.Alt) Then
            t = t & " Alt key pressed"
        End If
        lblModifierKey.Text = t
End Sub

Private Sub picLaSanta_MouseDown(ByVal sender As Object, _
    ByVal e As System.Windows.Forms.MouseEventArgs) _
    Handles picLaSanta.MouseDown
        display(sender, e)
End Sub

    Private Sub picLaSanta_MouseUp(ByVal sender As Object, _
    ByVal e As System.Windows.Forms.MouseEventArgs) _
    Handles picLaSanta.MouseUp
        display(sender, e)
End Sub

    Private Sub picLaSanta_MouseMove(ByVal sender As Object, _
    ByVal e As System.Windows.Forms.MouseEventArgs) _
    Handles picLaSanta.MouseMove
        display(sender, e)
End Sub
```

The X and Y co-ordinates of the position where the event occurred is given by using the **X** and **Y** properties of the **MouseEventArgs** object (called *e* in this application) which is passed to the method. Note that these co-ordinates give the position within the **PictureBox**, not within the container form.

The button which has been pressed is given by using the **Button** property. A check is made by comparing the value of this property to the **MouseButtons** enumeration, which can be either **Left**, **Middle**, **None**, **Right**, **XButton1** or **XButton2**.

The status of the Shift, Alt and Ctrl keys is found by performing the logical AND (using the & operator) on the **ModifierKeys** property of the **Control** class and the **Keys** enumeration. If this produces a **True** value that key has been pressed. Note that this application assumes that only one of these buttons has been pressed at any time.

MouseEnter and MouseLeave

These two events occur for a control when the mouse moves into a control and when it leaves it. It is the transition which occurs when the control border is crossed which causes these events.

Dragging and dropping

Dragging and dropping are the techniques used to move an item such as text from one position to another using the mouse. The item is selected and moved, keeping the button pressed. When the button is released the item is dropped into its new position.

To illustrate the dragging and dropping process we are going to look at an application shown running in Figure 14.4. Text can be selected in the top **TextBox** by clicking the left mouse button and dragging. The selected text can be dragged to the bottom **TextBox** by pressing the right mouse button while it is in the top **TextBox** and then moving the mouse to the bottom **TextBox** keeping that button pressed. If you attempt to drop the text anywhere else it will not do so. All of the text on the bottom **TextBox** is replaced by the dragged text.

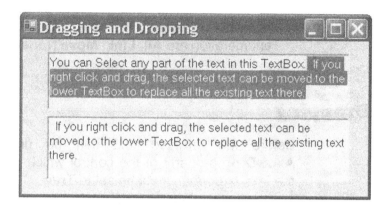

Figure 14.4 *Dragging and dropping text.*

Starting to drag

The drag event usually begins when the item to be dragged is clicked on. In this case when a mouse button is clicked in the top **TextBox** called *TxtTop*. The code for this event procedure is shown below:

```
Private Sub TxtTop_MouseDown(ByVal sender As Object, _
   ByVal e As System.Windows.Forms.MouseEventArgs) _
   Handles TxtTop.MouseDown
      If e.Button = MouseButtons.Right Then
          TxtTop.DoDragDrop(TxtTop.SelectedText, DragDropEffects.Copy)
      End If
End Sub
```

A check is made to see if it is the right button which has been pressed. If it has not no action is taken. If the right button has been pressed, the **DoDragDrop** method of the **TextBox** is used. This has two parameters:

- The text to be copied, in this case, the selected text.
- The permitted dragging operations which can occur in this case is copying. The other effects which are

available, listed in the **DragDropEffects** enumeration are **All**, **Link**, **Move None** and **Scroll**.

Dropping

Before the dragged text can be dropped, the **AllowDrop** property of the control which is to receive the text, *txtBottom*, must be set to **True**.

Two methods of the target control are required. The **DragEnter** method, is used to check that the data which is being dragged is a suitable type for dropping into the control.

```
Private Sub txtBottom_DragEnter(ByVal sender As Object, _
   ByVal e As System.Windows.Forms.DragEventArgs) _
   Handles txtBottom.DragEnter
      If e.Data.GetDataPresent(DataFormats.Text) Then
            e.Effect = DragDropEffects.Copy
      Else
            e.Effect = DragDropEffects.None
      End If
End Sub
```

In this case the only acceptable data type is text, if the dragged data is found to be anything else dropping is not permitted.

The **DragEventArgs** object, called *e* in this case, contains among other information the data which is being dragged.

The **Effects** property determines which drag and drop operations are allowed by the target.

The second method which must be considered is the **DragDrop** method for the target control. The code for this method is shown below:

```
Private Sub txtBottom_DragDrop(ByVal sender As Object, _
   ByVal e As System.Windows.Forms.DragEventArgs) _
```

```
Handles txtBottom.DragDrop
    txtBottom.Text = e.Data.GetData(DataFormats.Text).ToString( )
End Sub
```

The text displayed in the bottom **TextBox** called *txtBottom* is assigned the dragged text.

The **Data** property contains the data associated with the event. The **GetData** method returns the data which is being dragged. This method is passed a single parameter indicating the type of the data to be retrieved. This data is converted to a **String** by the **ToString** method.

The completed application is shown below:

```
Private Sub TxtTop_MouseDown(ByVal sender As Object, _
  ByVal e As System.Windows.Forms.MouseEventArgs) _
  Handles TxtTop.MouseDown
    If e.Button = MouseButtons.Right Then
        TxtTop.DoDragDrop(TxtTop.SelectedText, DragDropEffects.Copy)
    End If
End Sub

Private Sub txtBottom_DragEnter(ByVal sender As Object, _
  ByVal e As System.Windows.Forms.DragEventArgs) _
  Handles txtBottom.DragEnter
    If e.Data.GetDataPresent(DataFormats.Text) Then
        e.Effect = DragDropEffects.Copy
    Else
        e.Effect = DragDropEffects.None
    End If
End Sub

Private Sub txtBottom_DragDrop(ByVal sender As Object, _
  ByVal e As System.Windows.Forms.DragEventArgs) _
  Handles txtBottom.DragDrop
    txtBottom.Text = e.Data.GetData(DataFormats.Text).ToString( )
End Sub
```

Chapter 15

Databases and SQL

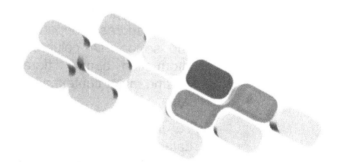

Introduction

Most professional applications have an underlying database, that is an extensive collection of information that can be viewed, altered and stored. In this chapter we are going to look at:

- What is SQL?
- Reading, amending and deleting records from a database.
- One to many relationships.

The Book database

In a relational database all information is stored in tables. Every row in a table contains information which relates to one item stored in the table, for example, if a table contained information on people working in a company, each row would contain information on one person. Typical information would include the person's name, address, department, phone number, e–mail and so on. A column contains the same type of information about different people, for example a column might contain all of the names of people in the table.

To illustrate this chapter we are going to use a database called *BookData* which has two tables: *Book* and *PublisherDetails*. You can create it using virtually any database system, but I have used Microsoft Access since this is very widely available.

Figure 15.1 shows the *Book* table with six rows of data, each corresponding to a book: the names of the fields are at the top of the column.

Book : Table

AuthorSurname	AuthorFirstName	Title	ISBN	Publisher
Mailer	Norman	The presidential papers	0-073-876433	Penguin
Blomfield	Louis	Twenty-hours	0-08-9984-54-2	Penguin
Blomfield	Louis	Mrs Parkington	0-08-9984-72-5	Penguin
Keenan	Brian	An evil cradling	0-09-99909-30	Delta
Rankin	Ian	Hide and seek	0-75280-941-5	Orion
Rankin	Ian	Knots and crosses	0-75280-942-3	Orion

Record: 7 of 7

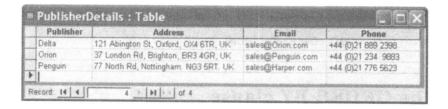

Figure 15.1 *The Book table.*

Figure 15.2 shows the *PublisherDetails* table and some data.

PublisherDetails : Table

Publisher	Address	Email	Phone
Delta	121 Abington St, Oxford, OX4 6TR, UK	sales@Orion.com	+44 (0)21 889 2398
Orion	37 London Rd, Brighton, BR3 4GR, UK	sales@Penguin.com	+44 (0)21 234 9883
Penguin	77 North Rd, Nottingham. NG3 5RT. UK	sales@Harper.com	+44 (0)21 776 5623

Record: 4 of 4

Figure 15.2 *The PublisherDetails table.*

These tables can be easily created in Access using the Wizards.

What is SQL?

SQL (Structured Query Language) is a language used by virtually every database to allow you to read and modify records, delete records and add new records.

Reading records

In SQL if you want to read records from a table you use a **SELECT** command of the form:

```
SELECT <field names> FROM <table name>
```

for example, if you had a table called *Books*, which contained information on authors such as their surname, the title of books they have written and their publishers, you could extract this information by specifying the names of the fields you wished to read:

```
SELECT AuthorSurname, Title, Publisher FROM Books
```

In this example A*uthorSurname, Title* and *Publisher* are the field names in the table called *Books*. If you wanted to read every field from the table you could use a * in place of the field names:

```
SELECT * FROM Books
```

The **SELECT** statement will return information for every row in the table.

The ORDER BY clause

You can control the order in which the records read from the database are displayed by adding an **ORDER BY** clause to the **SELECT** statement, for example:

```
SELECT AuthorSurname, Title FROM Books, Publisher ORDER BY Publisher
```

will return the information in alphabetical order. If the field which specifies the order is a number, the records are listed in ascending order.

You can sort by more than one field, for example:

```
SELECT AuthorSurname,Title FROM Books
ORDER BY Publisher, AuthorSurname
```

This command lists by *Publisher* and then orders the records relating to a particular publisher in alphabetical order of the *AuthorSurname*.

If you want to display records in reverse alphabetical order or in descending order for numeric fields you can place the **DESC** keyword after the field which orders the records returned, for example:

```
SELECT AuthorSurname, Title FROM Books ORDER BY AuthorSurname DESC
```

If you do not specify **DESC** the default **ASC** keyword is implied.

The WHERE clause

The **SELECT** statements we have seen so far return one record for every record in the table, however usually you only want to see records which match some specified criteria, for example:

```
SELECT Title FROM Books WHERE AuthorSurname = 'Blomfield'
```

This will display all of the books where the surname of the author is Blomfield. You can specify more than one **WHERE** clause:

```
SELECT Title FROM Books
WHERE AuthorSurname = 'Blomfield' AND 'AuthorFirstName = 'Louis'
```

and can also add an **OR** clause:

```
SELECT Title, AuthorSurname FROM Books
WHERE (AuthorSurname = 'Blomfield' AND 'AuthorFirstName = 'Louis')
    OR (AuthorSurname = 'Rankin' AND 'AuthorFirstName = 'Ian')
```

This will display the title and author surname for all of the books written by Louis Blomfield and Ian Rankin.

Modifying records

You can modify existing records using SQL with the **UPDATE** statement, which is of the form:

```
UPDATE <table name> SET <field name> = < value>
```

This will update all of the records in the table with the new value, so it is important to use the **WHERE** clause, for example:

```
UPDATE Books SET title = 'Twenty four hours'
WHERE title = 'Twenty hours'
```

You can update more than one field.

Deleting records

You can remove records from a table using the **DELETE** statement, which is of the form:

```
DELETE <table name> WHERE <conditions>
```

for example:

```
DELETE Books WHERE AuthorSurname = 'Rankin'
```

The **WHERE** clause can be as complex as you wish.

Adding records

You can add a new record into a table using the **INSERT INTO** statement, which is of the form:

```
INSERT INTO <table name> (field name1, field name2,..) VALUES
(value1,value2...)
```

for example:

```
INSERT INTO Books (AuthorSurname, AuthorFirstName, Title, ISBN, Publisher)
VALUES ('Hussain', 'Fiaz', 'Essential Flash', '0-887-9987-427', 'Springer')
```

It is important to make sure that the field names match the data values. If your table permits null entries in a field you can omit that field and a corresponding value.

One to many

Most databases have more than one table. It is essential that the tables are connected to each other by a common field, for example in our database the two tables have the *Publisher* field in common as shown in Figure 15.3.

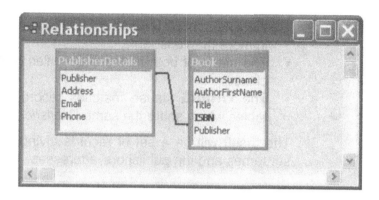

Figure 15.3 *Table relationships.*

In the *Book* table the ISBN is the primary key, that is, it contains a unique value which identifies one record. Similarly in the *PublisherDetails* table the *Publisher* field is the primary key. In the *Book* table, the *Publisher* field is not unique, but it does provide a link to the *Book* table. It is called a foreign key. Two tables are related when they are connected by a primary key in one table and a foreign key in another.

At first it may seem better in this database to simply include the publishers details in the *Book* table, but this would be very inefficient in terms of the space required. Each publisher may publish thousands of books, and it is far more space efficient to save the publisher details once rather than saving them repeatedly in every book. This type of relationship is called a one to many relationship.

You can write SQL SELECT statements for reading data from more than one table, for example:

```
SELECT Book.AuthorSurname, PublisherDetails.Address
FROM Book, PublisherDetails
WHERE Book.Publisher = PublisherDetails.Publisher
```

Note the following features:

- To refer to a field rather than just giving its name specify the name of the table, a period, and then the field name. The same field name may be found in more than one table.

- The name of both tables is specified in the **FROM** clause.
- The **WHERE** clause matches records in the two tables which share the same *Publisher*.

The result will be a set of records giving the authors' surnames and the publishers' addresses.

Chapter 16

The Data Form Wizard

Introduction

The Data Form Wizard is a flexible tool which helps you to write applications which reference databases. It produces forms which can carry out enquiries on databases, display the information they contain and update it if required.

In this chapter we are going to look at:

- What does the Data Form Wizard do?
- Running the Data Form Wizard.
- Connecting your application to a database.
- Reading, and editing a database.

What does the Wizard do?

The Data Form Wizard is a useful tool if you want a straightforward application. It is a good place to start if you are new to creating database applications. The wizard:

- Creates either a Web form page or Windows form.
- Adds the required data-bound controls to the form.
- Provides basic functionality for reading, and amending records.

The application we are going to develop reads an Access database and creates a Windows form, however reading other databases and creating a Web based form is a very similar.

The Data Form Wizard

To create this application you will need to create the *Books* database as described in the previous chapter or download it from the Essential Series web site *www.Essential-Series.com.*

- Start a Windows application in the usual way, called *Book.*
- Select the **Project | Add Component** menu option, select the **Data Form Wizard** icon and click **OK**.
- The welcome screen is displayed. Clicking on the **Next** Button displays the dialog shown in Figure 16.1.

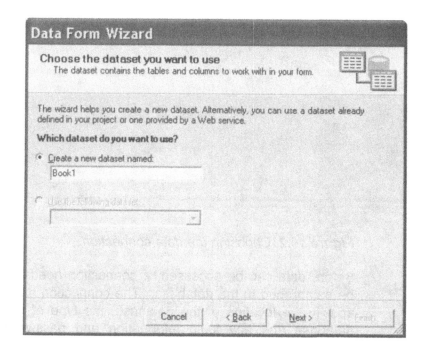

Figure 16.1 *Choosing the dataset.*

This dialog specifies the name of a dataset which holds the data fetched from the database after executing an SQL statement. The dataset is a collection of data in the form of tables with rows and columns which has been read from the data source. If you have already created a dataset you can use it, if not select **Create a new dataset named:** and specify the name *Book1.*

Click the **Next** button. The dialog shown in Figure 16.2 is displayed.

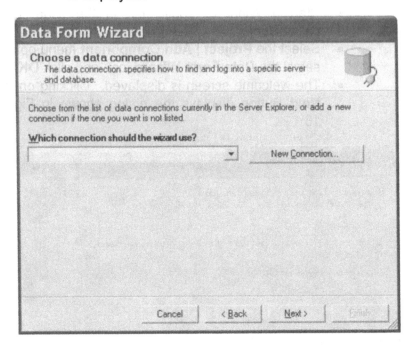

Figure 16.2 *Choosing the data connection.*

Before data can be accessed, a connection needs to be established to the database. The connection must specify the location of the database, the type of the database and any login information and password required.

To create a new connection click on the **New Connection** button to display the Data Link Properties dialog and click on the **Provider** tab to display the dialog shown in Figure 16.3.

This dialog allows you to specify the type of database you want to connect to. Since we are connecting to a local Access database, select the **Microsoft Jet 4.0 OLE DB Provider** option.

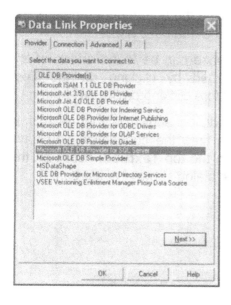

Figure 16.3 *Choosing the type of database.*

Click on the **Connection** tab to display the dialog shown in Figure 16.4.

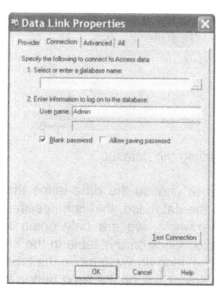

Figure 16.4 *Specifying the database location.*

This dialog is different depending on the provider you have selected. Enter the name of the database: you can browse by clicking on the button on the right of the **TextBox** provided for the database name.

Check that your database can be found and is of the type you have specified by clicking on the **Test Connection** button before clicking on the **OK** button.

The data connection dialog shown in Figure 16.1 is shown again, but this time the connection you have created is displayed in the top **TextBox**. Click on the **Next** button to see the dialog shown in Figure 16.5.

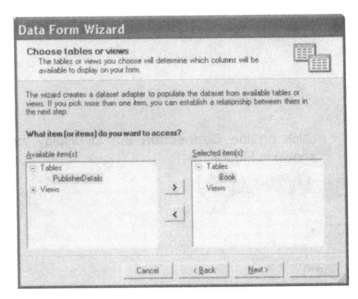

Figure 16.5 *Populating the dataset.*

This dialog allows you to choose the data items that you want to read from the database, that is it specifies the dataset. In this example, we are only going to reference the *Book* table. Click on this table in the left Box and click the right pointing arrow to move the table to the **Selected items** Box. Click on the **Next** button to specify the dialog shown in Figure 16.6.

The dialog allows you to choose the columns of data which are to be displayed. If you had chosen to display information from more than one table, you would have to choose the data to display from the second table. In this case select all of the columns for display as shown in Figure 16.6.

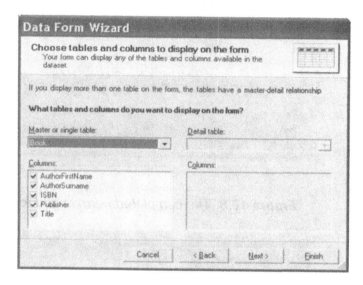

Figure 16.6 *Selecting data for display.*

Click on **Next** to show the dialog shown in Figure 16.7.

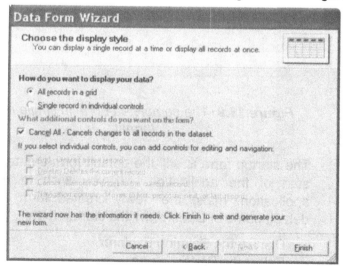

Figure 16.7 *Selecting data for display.*

The data may be displayed in different formats, these are both shown in Figures 16.8 and 16.9. Click on the **Finish** button to end the Wizard.

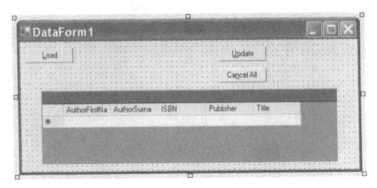

Figure 16.8 The completed Form in grid format.

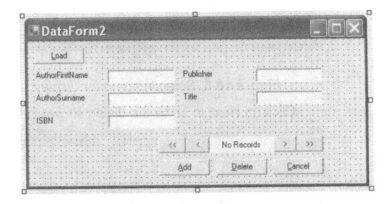

Figure 16.9 The completed Form in single record format.

The startup form is still the default form created at the start of the application. If you wish to test the application, make the newly created form, with its default name of *DataForm1* the startup form:

- Display the Solution Explorer.
- Select the Project name.

- Select the **Project | Properties** menu option to display the Property Pages dialog.
- Change the Startup object to **DataForm1**.
- Click on **OK**.

The control which is used to display the information is a **DataGrid**.

The size of the area occupied by the **DataGrid** is controlled by the **Size** property. The width of the columns is determined by the **PreferredColumnWidth** property. At run-time you can alter the width of columns manually by dragging on the vertical bar between columns.

The running application is shown in Figure 16.10.

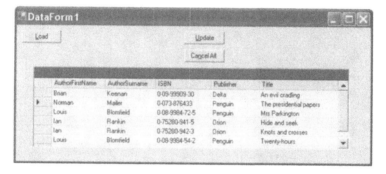

Figure 16.10 *The running application in grid format.*

To read data from the database, click the **Load** button. If you wish to change any data you can edit the grid, but the changes are not saved until you press the **Update** button.

For many straightforward database systems you can use the Visual Data Manager or the Data Form Wizard, but if you want total control over your database applications you need to write the application yourself using data–bound controls and SQL queries.

Chapter 17

DataReader and DataSet

Introduction

If you are developing a simple database application you may find that the database Forms Wizard will give you the functionality you need, but if not, you will have to write some Visual Basic code to specify exactly what you want. This is a huge area and therefore the coverage in this chapter is only intended as an introduction on how to connect your application to a database and read data using the **OleDbDataReader** and **DataSet** classes. It does not cover editing and updating databases. In this chapter we are going to look at:

- Connecting to a database.
- Using the **OleDbDataReader** class to read data.
- Using the **DataSet** class to read from a database.

Reading the Book database

The Windows application we are going to develop opens the *Books* database and reads the records one at a time.

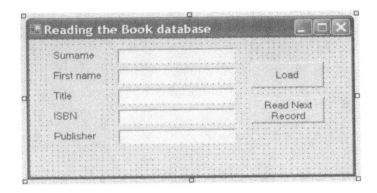

Figure 17.1 *The application at design-time.*

The completed application at design-time is shown in Figure 17.1. If you want to try this or the following application for yourself you must specify the location of your copy of the *Book* database on your computer, rather than the location used in this chapter.

Clicking on the *Load* button connects to the database and clicking on the *Read Next Record* button displays records in sequence until the end of the file is reached.

- Start a new Windows application.
- Create the user interface shown in Figure17.1.
- Rename the **Button** controls *btnLoad* and *btnRead*.
- Rename the **TextBox** controls *txtAuthorSurname*, *txtAuthorFirstName*, *txtTitle*, *txtISBN*, *txtPublisher*.

The next stage is to connect to the database.

Connecting to the database

To connect to the database we need to create an instance of the **OleDbConnection** class, and to pass it the information required to establish the connection, such as the type of database and any logon information which is required.

The connection required for our Access database is defined below:

```
Private Const strConnection As String = "Provider=Microsoft.Jet.OLEDB.4.0; " &_
Data Source=C:\BOOKS\VB\VBNet\BookData.mdb;Persist Security Info=False"
```

This is passed to the constructor of the **OleDbConnection** object:

```
Dim objConnection As New _
  System.Data.OleDb.OleDbConnection(strConnection)
```

This provides a connection to the database. It is easy to make a mistake when creating the connection string, especially if you are using a SQL database which is more complicated. There is an indirect way of creating this **String**:

- Display the Desktop.
- Right click and select the **New | Text Document** option.
- Rename this file so that it has an extension of .udl.
- Double click on this file to display the Data Link properties dialog and click on the **Provider** tag as shown in Figure 16.3 in Chapter 16.
- Select the type of database from the **Provider** page and then specify the connection aspects such as the database location and name on the **Connection** page.
- Finally open the .udl file with a text editor such as Notepad to cut the connection string which has been produced and paste this back into your application, remembering to place it in quotes.

The actual connection to the database is done with **Open** method of the **OleDbConnection** object:

```
objConnection.Open( )
```

SQL statements

To read from the database now that the connection has been established we need to create an **OleDbCommand** object. The SQL statement to be executed is created as a **String** and passed to the new **OleDbCommand** constructor along with the name of the **OleDbConnection** object:

```
Private Const strSQL As String = "SELECT * FROM book"
Dim objcommand As New _
   System.Data.OleDb.OleDbCommand(strSQL, objConnection)
```

The SQL is executed by the **ExecuteReader** method of the **OleDbCommand** object and the result is returned in an **OleDbDataReader** object:

```
Dim objReader As System.Data.OleDb.OleDbDataReader
objReader = objcommand.ExecuteReader( )
```

To extract the individual fields from the **OleDbDataReader** object, the **GetString** method is used, for example, **objReader.GetString**(0) is the first field, the author surname. There are other methods available, for example, reading a data item of another type such as an integer.

The complete application is shown below:

```
Private Const strConnection As String = "Provider=Microsoft.Jet.OLEDB.4.0; " &_
"Data Source=C:\BOOKS\VB\VBNet\BookData.mdb;Persist Security Info=False"
Private Const strSQL As String = "SELECT * FROM book"
Dim objConnection As New _
   System.Data.OleDb.OleDbConnection(strConnection)
Dim objcommand As New _
   System.Data.OleDb.OleDbCommand(strSQL, objConnection)
Dim objReader As System.Data.OleDb.OleDbDataReader

Private Sub btnLoad_Click(ByVal sender As System.Object, _
   ByVal e As System.EventArgs) Handles btnLoad.Click
      objConnection.Open( )
      objReader = objcommand.ExecuteReader( )
End Sub

Private Sub btnRead_Click(ByVal sender As System.Object, _
   ByVal e As System.EventArgs) Handles btnRead.Click
      If objConnection.State = ConnectionState.Open Then
         If objReader.Read( ) Then
               txtAuthorSurname.Text = objReader.GetString(0)
               txtAuthorFirstName.Text = objReader.GetString(1)
               txtTitle.Text = objReader.GetString(2)
               txtISBN.Text = objReader.GetString(3)
               txtPublisher.Text = objReader.GetString(4)
         Else : MessageBox.Show("End of File", "DataReader")
               Application.Exit( )
         End If
      End If
End Sub
```

The running application is shown in Figure 17.2.

The application in its present form is easily crashed, but it is straightforward to add some error checking.

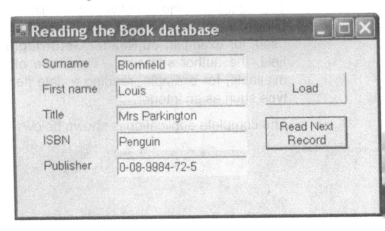

Figure 17.2 *The application at run-time.*

Error checking

Error checking is especially important when writing database applications, since problems frequently occur, for example, trying to connect to a database when a connection has already been made, or attempting to read from a database when there is no connection. The addition of a few **Try** and **Catch** clauses can satisfactorily handle these types of errors, for example:

```
Try
    objConnection.Open( )
    Catch ex As System.Exception
        MessageBox.Show("Error opening database", "DataReader")
        Application.Exit( )
End Try
```

If the connection cannot be made, an exception is produced; the **Catch** clause is executed; an error dialog is displayed and the application ends.

Try Catch clauses should be used in a similar way with methods which read data. A revised version of the application with this and some additional error checking is shown below:

```
Private Const strConnection As String = "Provider=Microsoft.Jet.OLEDB.4.0;" & _
"Data Source=C:\BOOKS\VB\VBNet\BookData.mdb;Persist Security Info=False"
Private Const strSQL As String = "SELECT * FROM book"
Dim objConnection As New _
System.Data.OleDb.OleDbConnection(strConnection)
Dim objcommand As New _
System.Data.OleDb.OleDbCommand(strSQL, objConnection)
Dim objReader As System.Data.OleDb.OleDbDataReader

Private Sub btnLoad_Click(ByVal sender As System.Object, _
    ByVal e As System.EventArgs) Handles btnLoad.Click
        If objConnection.State = ConnectionState.Closed Then
            Try
                    objConnection.Open( )
                    Catch ex As System.Exception
                    MessageBox.Show("Error opening database", "DataReader")
                        Application.Exit( )
            End Try
            objReader = objcommand.ExecuteReader( )
        End If
End Sub

Private Sub btnRead_Click(ByVal sender As System.Object, _
    ByVal e As System.EventArgs) Handles btnRead.Click
        If objConnection.State = ConnectionState.Open Then
            Try
                    If objReader.Read( ) Then
                        txtAuthorSurname.Text = objReader.GetString(0)
                        txtAuthorFirstName.Text = objReader.GetString(1)
                        txtTitle.Text = objReader.GetString(2)
                        txtISBN.Text = objReader.GetString(3)
                        txtPublisher.Text = objReader.GetString(4)
                    Else : MessageBox.Show("End of File", "DataReader")
                        Application.Exit( )
                    End If
            Catch ex As System.Exception
                    MessageBox.Show("Error reading database", "DataReader")
                    Application.Exit( )
```

```
            End Try
        End If
    End Sub
```

This completes the application, but there are a few problems with using the **OleDbDataReader** class: the data is read only and can only be read sequentially from the start to the end of the database. If the **DataSet** class is used, a snapshot of the data is taken, and the connection to the database may then be broken and the data manipulated locally. If the **OleDbDataReader** class is used a constant connection to the database must be maintained. In the next section we are going to look at how the **DataSet** class can be used to read data from a database.

The DataSet class

The **DataSet** class provides an alternative way of working with data: instead of maintaining a connection to the database, the information is downloaded to the local computer. Immediately the data has been read the connection to the database may be broken.

In the next application we are going to look at how a dataset is created and the information it contains displayed. It is visually the same as the previous application, shown in Figures 17.1 and 17.2, however the supporting code is very different.

An application using DataSet class

The running application we are going to develop is shown in Figure 17.3. In addition to buttons for loading and reading forwards sequentially through the database, you can read backwards and also move directly to the first and last records.

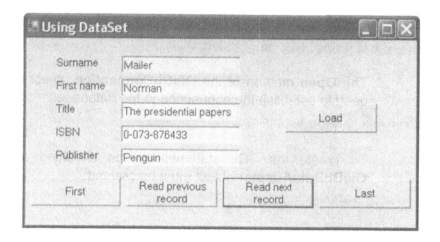

Figure 17.3 *The application at run-time.*

To create this application:

- Start a new Windows application and then create the user interface.
- Change the names of the **TextBox** controls to txtAuthorSurname, txtAuthorFirstName, txtTitle, txtISBN, and txtPublisher.
- Rename the **Button** controls: *btnFirst*, *btnPrevious*, *btnRead* and *btnLast*.

As before the next stage is to connect to the database.

Connecting to the database

The process is the same as for the previous example using a **OleDbDataReader** object:

The connection string is defined:

```
Private Const strConnection As String = _
  "Provider=Microsoft.Jet.OLEDB.4.0; Data Source=C:\BOOKS\VB\VBNet" & _
  "\BookData.mdb;Persist Security Info=False"
```

An **OleDbConnection** object is created and passed the connection **String**:

```
Dim objConnection As New _
    System.Data.OleDb.OleDbConnection(strConnection)
```

The **Open** method of the **OleDbConnection** object is used to establish the connection to the database:

```
objConnection.Open( )
```

To create the SQL statement to be executed an **OleDbDataAdapter** object must be created:

```
Private Const strSQL As String = "SELECT * FROM book"
Dim objDataAdapter As _
    New OleDb.OleDbDataAdapter(strSQL, objConnection)
```

This object is passed the SQL query and the **OleDbConnection** object.

Everything is now ready to execute the SQL, read from the database and populate the data set.

Reading from the database

To read from the database a **DataSet** object must be created:

```
Dim objDataSet As New DataSet( )
```

The **Fill** method of the **OleDbDataAdapter** is used to read from the database and to put data into the **DataSet** object:

```
objDataAdapter.Fill(objDataSet, "AllBooks")
```

The **DataSet** created can be referred to by the specified name: *AllBooks*.

Using the DataSet class

The **DataSet** object now contains the results of the SQL query and the connection between the database and the application can be closed, since the required data is now stored locally and can be referenced without reference to the database:

```
objConnection.Close( )
```

To use the data in the **DataSet** object the **Tables** collection is used, for example the number of records in the **DataSet** is given by:

```
objDataSet.Tables("AllBooks").Rows.Count
```

If you want to access the data in the **DataSet** object this must be transferred into a **DataTable** object. This object has two collections:

- The **Rows** collection contains all of the rows in the **DataTable** object. Each row is stored as a **DataRow** object.
- The **Column** collection contains a description of each of the columns in the **DataTable** object. Each field description is stored as a **DataColumn** object.

The **DataTable** object can be instantiated and populated as shown:

```
Dim objTable As DataTable
objTable = objDataSet.Tables("AllBooks")
```

Note that the **Tables** method is passed the name of the **DataSet** *AllBooks*.

The individual items from the **DataSet** can be read using the **Items** property, for example to read the field called *AuthorSurname* from the first row (indicated by a zero in brackets after **Row**):

```
objTable.Rows(0).Item("AuthorSurname")
```

This is a **String** which can be displayed in any compatible control such as a **TextBox**.

The completed application

In the completed application, the **Load** button event handler establishes the connection to the database and populates the **DataSet** and the **DataTable**.

The completed application with some error handling included is shown below:

```vb
Private Const strConnection As String = _
    "Provider=Microsoft.Jet.OLEDB.4.0; Data Source=C:\BOOKS\VB\VBNet" & _
    "\BookData.mdb;Persist Security Info=False"
Private Const strSQL As String = "SELECT * FROM book"
Dim objConnection As New _
    System.Data.OleDb.OleDbConnection(strConnection)
Dim objDataAdapter As _
    New OleDb.OleDbDataAdapter(strSQL, objConnection)
Dim objDataSet As New DataSet( )
Dim objTable As DataTable
Dim objRow As DataRow
Dim c As Integer = -1

Private Sub btnLoad_Click(ByVal sender As System.Object, _
    ByVal e As System.EventArgs) Handles btnLoad.Click
        If objConnection.State = ConnectionState.Closed Then
            objConnection.Open( )
            objDataAdapter.Fill(objDataSet, "AllBooks")
        End If
        objConnection.Close( )
        objTable = objDataSet.Tables("AllBooks")
End Sub

Private Sub btnRead_Click(ByVal sender As System.Object, _
    ByVal e As System.EventArgs) Handles btnRead.Click
        c = c + 1
        Try
            If (c < objDataSet.Tables("AllBooks").Rows.Count) Then
        Call readRecord( )
            Else :c = 0
                Call readRecord( )
        End If
```

```
        Catch ex As system.Exception
            MessageBox.Show("Error opening database", "DataSet")
        End Try
End Sub

Private Sub btnPrevious_Click(ByVal sender As System.Object, _
    ByVal e As System.EventArgs) Handles btnPrevious.Click
        If c <> 0 Then
            c = c - 1
        Else
            c = objDataSet.Tables("AllBooks").Rows.Count - 1
        End If
        Call readRecord( )
End Sub

Private Sub btnFirst_Click(ByVal sender As System.Object, _
    ByVal e As System.EventArgs) Handles btnFirst.Click
        c = 0
        Call readRecord( )
End Sub

Private Sub btnLast_Click(ByVal sender As System.Object, _
    ByVal e As System.EventArgs) Handles btnLast.Click
        Try
            c = objDataSet.Tables("AllBooks").Rows.Count - 1
        Catch ex As system.Exception
            MessageBox.Show("Error reading database", "DataSet")
        End Try
        Call readRecord( )
End Sub

Private Sub readRecord( )
        Try
            txtAuthorSurname.Text = objTable.Rows(c).Item("AuthorSurname")
            txtAuthorFirstName.Text = objTable.Rows(c).Item("AuthorFirstName")
            txtTitle.Text = objTable.Rows(c).Item("Title")
            txtISBN.Text = objTable.Rows(c).Item("ISBN")
            txtPublisher.Text = objTable.Rows(c).Item("Publisher")
        Catch ex As System.Exception
            MessageBox.Show("Error reading database", "DataSet")
        End Try
End Sub
```

The reading of the **DataTable** object is performed in the *readRecord* procedure which reads the record indicated by the variable called *c*. The individual fields of that row are copied the **Text** property of **TextBox** controls for display.

- Reading the first record simply sets the value of c to zero and calls the *readRecord* procedure.
- Reading the last record sets *c* to the number of records in the table minus 1 (since the first record is zero).
- Reading the next and previous records increases or decreases *c* by 1.
- If the intended record to be read is past the end of the table, the first record is read, similarly if that record is before the start of the table the last record is read.

Index

The Essential Series

Editor: John Cowell

If you are looking for an accessible and quick introduction to a new language or area then these are the books for you.

Covering a wide range of topics including virtual reality, computer animation, Java, and Visual Basic to name but a few, the books provide a quick and accessible introduction to the subject. **Essential** books let you start developing your own applications with the minimum of fuss - and fast.

All books are, of course, available from all good booksellers (who can order them even if they are not in stock), but if you have difficulties you can contact the publishers direct, by telephoning +44 1483 418822
(in the UK and Europe), +1/212/4 60 15 00 (in the USA),
or by emailing orders@svl.co.uk

www.springer.co.uk   www.springer.de
www.springer-ny.com

Essential
Visual Basic 6.0 *fast*

John Cowell

Visual Basic is a mature and powerful, integrated development environment which allows you to create professional Windows applications. It has an intuitive user interface, an extensive set of components and excellent debugging facilities, so, whether you are a professional programmer or a student, this book tells you everything you need to know to write professional applications for Windows using Visual Basic 6.0.

Version 6.0 is the latest version of Visual Basic and includes all of the facilities of earlier versions combined with an extensive set of new controls. These greatly extend the capabilities for writing database and web-based applications.

Once you've read this book, you'll know all about:
- The Visual Basic language.
- The standard Visual Basic controls.
    - Handling control events.
    - Using data aware controls.
    - Creating and using ActiveX controls.
    - Writing web-based applications.

Essential Visual Basic 6.0 fast is designed for professional developers and students who need to learn the maximum in the minimum time and to develop applications *fast*.

224 pages
Softcover
ISBN 1-85233-207-7

Please see page 251 for ordering details

Essential C#
fast

Ian Chivers

Essential C# *fast* is a quick, practical introduction to
the C# programming language.

In this book you will learn about:

- Using C# with a traditional compile run cycle;
- Using C# within the Developer Studio
  environment;
- Different data types supported in C#;
- Control structures and input and output
  (i/o) in C#;
- Key features of C# and their relationship to C,
  C++, Java, and other programming languages.

This is one of the first introductory books on C# and
includes lots of clear simple examples, highlighting
the core features of the language.

280 pages
Softcover
ISBN 1-85233-562-9

Please see page 251 for ordering details